LIVING Our FAITH

Church History
Our Christian Story

Principal **Consultants**

Dennis J. Bozanich, MBA

Michael Carotta, EdD

Rev. Leonard Wenke, MDiv

Principal **Reviewers**

Mary Lee Becker, MPM

Robert J. Kealey, EdD

M. Annette Mandley-Turner, MS

Harcourt
Religion Publishers

Nihil Obstat
Rev. Richard L. Schaefer
Censor Deputatus

Imprimatur
✠ Most Rev. Jerome Hanus, OSB
Archbishop of Dubuque
January 31, 2001
Feast of Saint John Bosco, Patron of Youth and Catholic Publishers

The nihil obstat and imprimatur are official declarations that a book or pamphlet is free of doctrinal or moral error. No implication is contained herein that those who granted the nihil obstat and imprimatur agree with the contents, opinions, or statements expressed.

Our Mission
The primary mission of Harcourt Religion Publishers is to provide the Catholic and Christian educational markets with the highest quality catechetical print and media resources. The content of these resources reflects the best insights of current theology, methodology, and pedagogical research. These resources are practical and easy to use, designed to meet expressed market needs, and written to reflect the teachings of the Catholic Church.

Photography Credits
Art Resource: Giraudon: 58, 68; Erich Lessing: 15, 16, 38, 48; National Musuem of American Art, Washington DC: 88; Scala: 66; Victoria & Albert Museum, London: 27; **Bridgeman Art Library:** Baptistery, Florence, Italy: 102; Basilica of St. John, Ayasoluk, Ephesus, Turkey: 36; Bibliotheque Nationale, Paris, France: 64; Phillips, The International Fine Art Auctioneers, UK: 57; Peter Willi/Louvre, Paris, France: 37; **British Library Sloane:** 2435, fol. 85; by permission: 47; **Catholic News Service:** 88, Lisa Kessler: 19; **The Rev. Dr. David Cottrill:** 35; **Christie's Images, LTD.:** 26, 67; **Corbis:** 26; G. E. Kidder Smith: 78; Vittoriano Rastelli: 8; **FPG International:** Mike Malyszko: 51; Telegraph Colour Library: 4, 7; Arthur Tilley: 11; **Jim France Photography:** Jim France: 75; **Jack Holtel:** 14, 18, 28, 39, 40, 54, 60, 70, 84; **Image Bank:** Rob Atkins: 76, 78; Ken Huang: 40; **Impact Visuals:** Bruce Paton: 85; **Index Stock Imagery:** 65, Carlene W. Smith: 76; **Liaison International:** Kathleen Campbell: 47; Kermni: 80; Kurgan-Lisnet: 40; Stephanie Pert: 46; **David Madison Sports Images:** David Madison: 94; **Natural Bridges:** 26; Robert Lentz: 78; **Nicholas Studios:** Nick Falzerano: 20; **North Wind Picture Archives:** 74; **Photo Edit:** Phil Borden: 100; Myrleen Ferguson Cate: 83; Richard Hutchings: 44; Michael Newman: 30; A. Ramey: 77; **Picture Quest:** Ann Purcell & Carl Purcell: 100; Alon Reininger/Contact Press Images: 96; **Skjold Photographs:** 70, 95; **Stock Boston:** 77, Bachman: 40; Micheal A. Dwyer: 100; Dorothy Littell Greco: 32; Rhonda Sidney: 92; **The Stock Market:** Ken Straito: 37; **Stone:** Oliver Benn: 101; Wayne Eastep: 100; Robert Frerck: 34; David Young-Wolff: 5; **Superstock:** 16, 26, 30, 44, 56, 89, 90, 97, 101; A.K.G., Berlin: 56; Christie's Images: 10; Musee du Louvre, Paris: 69; **Unicorn Stock Photos:** Florent Flipper: 87; **Visuals Unlimited:** Donna Caldwell: 77; Jeff Greenberg: 40; **W. P. Wittman Photography:** Bill Wittman: 6; **Wonderfile:** 98

Cover Photos
AGI Photographic Imaging; The Crosiers: Gene Plaisted

Feature Icons
Catholics Believe: Jack Holtel; **Opening the Word:** PictureQuest; **Our Christian Journey:** PictureQuest: Chuck Fishman/Contact Press Images

Location and Props
Dayton Church Supply; St. Christopher Catholic School, Vandalia, OH; St. Peter Catholic School, Huber Heights, OH

Skills for Christian Living
The skill steps in Reconciling, and the Name It, Tame It, Claim It process, both from the *Catholic and Capable* series, are used with permission from Resources for Christian Living.

Printed in the United States of America

ISBN 0-15-900518-3

LIVING Our FAITH
Church History
Our Christian Story

I Believe

God our Father, we thank you for the life you have given us. Help us follow the teachings of Jesus your Son and our Savior. May your Holy Spirit help us live in relationship with you and care for your Church. Amen.

Take a few minutes to sketch three objects or symbols that remind you of Christian beliefs.

Choose one of the objects or symbols you sketched, and tell which belief it reminds you of and why it is important to you to make that connection.

_____

_____

_____

Our Stories,
Our Lives

Think about the story of your life. What are the most important things that have happened to you? What are some of your dreams for the future? Each of us has a personal story—a combination of the events that we have experienced, the people who have touched our lives, and our hopes for tomorrow.

Each person's story is unique. But our lives are connected to and supported by the lives of many other people. Our relationships help form and guide who we are. The people close to us are an important part of our personal stories, and we are part of their stories. As Christians we are also connected to each other through the Church. Our personal stories are part of the ongoing Christian story.

The Apostles' Mission

Imagine an experience that could change your life. Suppose that a teacher you love and respect has chosen you to do a difficult job, one that will put you in the position of being laughed at, criticized, and rejected by your classmates—and even by your family. You want to do the job. But doing it makes every day a challenge, and very few people understand what you are doing or why.

That is what Jesus' **apostles** faced. They were pioneers in the faith, carrying the news of God's saving love to the ends of the earth, teaching and healing in his name. Jesus knew that the apostles would face many hardships and that many people would hear the gospel message as a threat to their way of life. Jesus promised his followers that he would send the Holy Spirit to strengthen and encourage them.

The first followers of Jesus, who were Jewish, didn't think they were starting a new religion. They read Scripture and prayed with the rest of the Jewish community. For these earliest followers, believing in Jesus and following his teachings was their way of being Jewish. Fifty days after Jesus was raised from the dead, the friends of Jesus gathered together on the Jewish day of **Pentecost,** which celebrates the covenant agreement between God and the Jewish people. Suddenly, the Holy Spirit came into their midst and gave them the gifts they would need to carry out the mission of Jesus.

Strengthened by the Holy Spirit with courage and wisdom, the apostles and other **disciples** traveled to many places to share their faith in Jesus Christ. These followers of Jesus lived his teachings and helped others understand who Jesus was and how he could change their lives. They called people to repent, turn back to God, and be baptized.

Opening the Word

4th Sunday of Easter, Cycle A

Peter said to them, "Repent, and be baptized every one of you in the name of Jesus Christ so that your sins may be forgiven; and you will receive the gift of the Holy Spirit."
Acts 2:38

Read *Acts 2:37–42* as well as *1 Corinthians 2:12–15* and *Ephesians 3:16–17.* Who can receive the gift of the Holy Spirit?

_____

_____

Christians in
Community

Christianity is the religion of those who follow Christ and his teachings. Because of our Baptism the story of Christianity is our story, too, and its mission is our mission. Our Christian story is one of community. The early Christians took care of one another, showed particular concern for widows and orphans, and shared food and clothing with those who needed them. They retold the story of Jesus and listened to the Jewish Scriptures and the letters of the apostles. They thanked God and broke bread together in Jesus' name.

We share the same faith in Jesus Christ, our savior, who reconciled all humanity with God. We celebrate all that he did for us through his life, suffering, death, and resurrection. We still gather to pray, listen to Scripture, and break bread together in his name, as he told us to do.

Some of the disciples of Jesus traveled the extensive network of Roman roads to the far corners of the empire to spread his message. Some sailed to ports around the Mediterranean Sea to preach the good news to the Jewish communities there.

Christian Roots in Jerusalem

For the earliest Christians the city of Jerusalem was the center of community life. Scripture tells us that the first leader of the Church in Jerusalem was the apostle James the Greater. He was related to Jesus and guided the small community in its early days. From Jerusalem the Christian message spread to cities around the Mediterranean Sea and in the Middle East.

In A.D. 66 the Jewish people revolted against the Romans. And in A.D. 70 the Romans destroyed the temple in Jerusalem. That date marked an important turning point in Jewish and Christian history, as many members of both groups began to move out of Palestine, the Roman name for Israel. Jerusalem ceased to be a center of Christian life. Eventually, Christianity was no longer considered part of the Jewish faith.

For further information: Use an encyclopedia to find out more about the destruction and fall of Jerusalem.

	25	75
43 CITY OF LONDON FOUNDED		
49 COUNCIL OF JERUSALEM MEETS		
54-68 REIGN OF NERO, ROMAN EMPEROR		
c.58-c.75 MING TI, THE CHINESE EMPEROR, INTRODUCES BUDDHISM TO CHINA		
70 DESTRUCTION OF THE TEMPLE IN JERUSALEM		

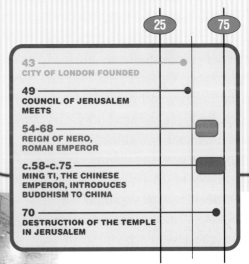

Jerusalem is a rich tapestry of modern buildings, ancient city walls and ruins, and religious sites that are sacred to Christians, Jews, and Muslims.

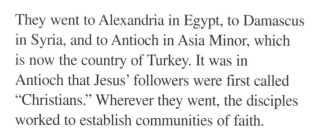

The current bishops are the successors of the apostles.
See Catechism, #77.

What is one way that you share the bishops' responsibility for carrying on the mission of the apostles and spreading the good news?

_____

_____

Share your thoughts with your Faith Partner. FaiTH ParTNeRSHiP

They went to Alexandria in Egypt, to Damascus in Syria, and to Antioch in Asia Minor, which is now the country of Turkey. It was in Antioch that Jesus' followers were first called "Christians." Wherever they went, the disciples worked to establish communities of faith.

Issues and Answers

As people who were not Jewish heard about Jesus, they also became interested in him. Disagreements developed about whether these non-Jewish people, called **Gentiles,** had to become Jewish to join the Christian community. Other disputes focused on whether or not Jesus was the messiah for whom many of the Jews had been waiting. Over time, such disagreements would lead to Christians leaving or being forced out of the Jewish communities. Can you think of a time when a group of people at your school wouldn't let a certain person join the group? How was this situation resolved?

Each new community of Christians had unique strengths and needs. The apostles appointed leaders to guide the communities in using their gifts and in meeting the community's needs. The apostles and other leaders eventually met in Jerusalem to address some of the issues that Christians were facing. In *Acts 15:1–35* we read about this first official Church meeting, called the **Council of Jerusalem,** which was held around A.D. 49, about fifteen years after Jesus' death and resurrection.

Those who attended the meeting decided that Gentiles did not have to become Jewish in order to follow Jesus—faith in Jesus was the only requirement. The Church leaders then sent a letter explaining their decision to the other Christian communities.

Throughout the centuries the Church has held many councils to decide matters of faith, teaching, and practice. The most recent Church council was the Second Vatican Council, which is often referred to as Vatican II. The work of this council, which was held in Rome between 1962 and 1965, was to help the Church speak in a way that could be better understood in the modern world.

Today we try, as the early Christians did, to live as a community of Jesus' followers. As members of the twenty-first century Church, we work out ways to take care of one another and share what we have with those in need. When issues come up that affect the life of the Church and its people, our bishops meet to discuss the situation and offer guidance that helps us continue to grow in faith and love.

Jesus' Return

Many early followers of Jesus believed that he would return very soon, and they expected that the end of the world would happen at that time. But as the first generation of Jesus' followers began to age and die, some Christians wrote down what they had seen or heard. They realized that the end of the world might not happen as soon as they had expected, and they wanted to record their experience of Jesus.

One writer, who called himself John, wrote the Book of Revelation, the last book of the Bible. Revelation promises that God will bring about a new creation, a time of fulfillment, at the end of time. The writer reported an amazing vision of symbols and numbers that conveyed messages to seven churches in Asia Minor. Some of these symbols can be confusing to us, but they would have been helpful to early Christians who were being persecuted. Throughout the book, one promise appears again and again: God will soon triumph over evil. The Book of Revelation ends with a prayer, "Come, Lord Jesus!"

Media Message

LIFE STORIES A biography, the story of someone's life, gives us a window into another person's experience. Life stories can inspire and encourage us. Through a book or video of a saint or another person of faith, we can discover how that person's beliefs affected his or her life.

Use the space below to tell whose life story you would like to read, and explain why.

_____

_____

_____

_____

On with **the Story**

Our Christian faith is based on a personal relationship with Jesus that is expressed in community. Learning more about our ancestors in the faith and their experiences of God can help us grow in our Christian relationships. As the early Christians met, prayed, and celebrated, they experienced a joy that spread to others in their families and communities. The life and traditions of those early Christian communities became the first chapter of our ongoing Christian story.

Our lives sometimes seem complicated and confusing. As we grow in our faith, we discover that our relationship with Jesus can make a positive difference. Through the centuries the Church has provided a way for us to celebrate and strengthen that relationship. The Holy Spirit guides the Church and gives us the courage to live as disciples of Jesus.

Our Christian story is a story of love— God's love for us, our love for God, and our love for one another. It is also a story of challenging the culture to a new understanding of itself. It's a very old story, but it isn't finished yet. How we live each day is an important part of this story. What we learn from the early Christian community can help guide us as the living Church today.

Reflect on how our relationship with Jesus affects our relationship with the Church. Share your thoughts with your Faith Partner.

FaiTH PaRTNeRSHiP

WRAP UP

- •Jesus gave his apostles the mission to spread the good news of God's kingdom throughout the world.
- •On the Jewish festival of Pentecost, the Holy Spirit came into the midst of the followers of Jesus.
- •At the Council of Jerusalem, the early Christian leaders decided that Gentiles could become Christians without becoming Jewish first.
- •At first the early Christians believed that Jesus would return very soon.
- •Today we have the same faith in Jesus that the first Christians had.

What questions do you have about the content of this chapter?

_____

_____

_____

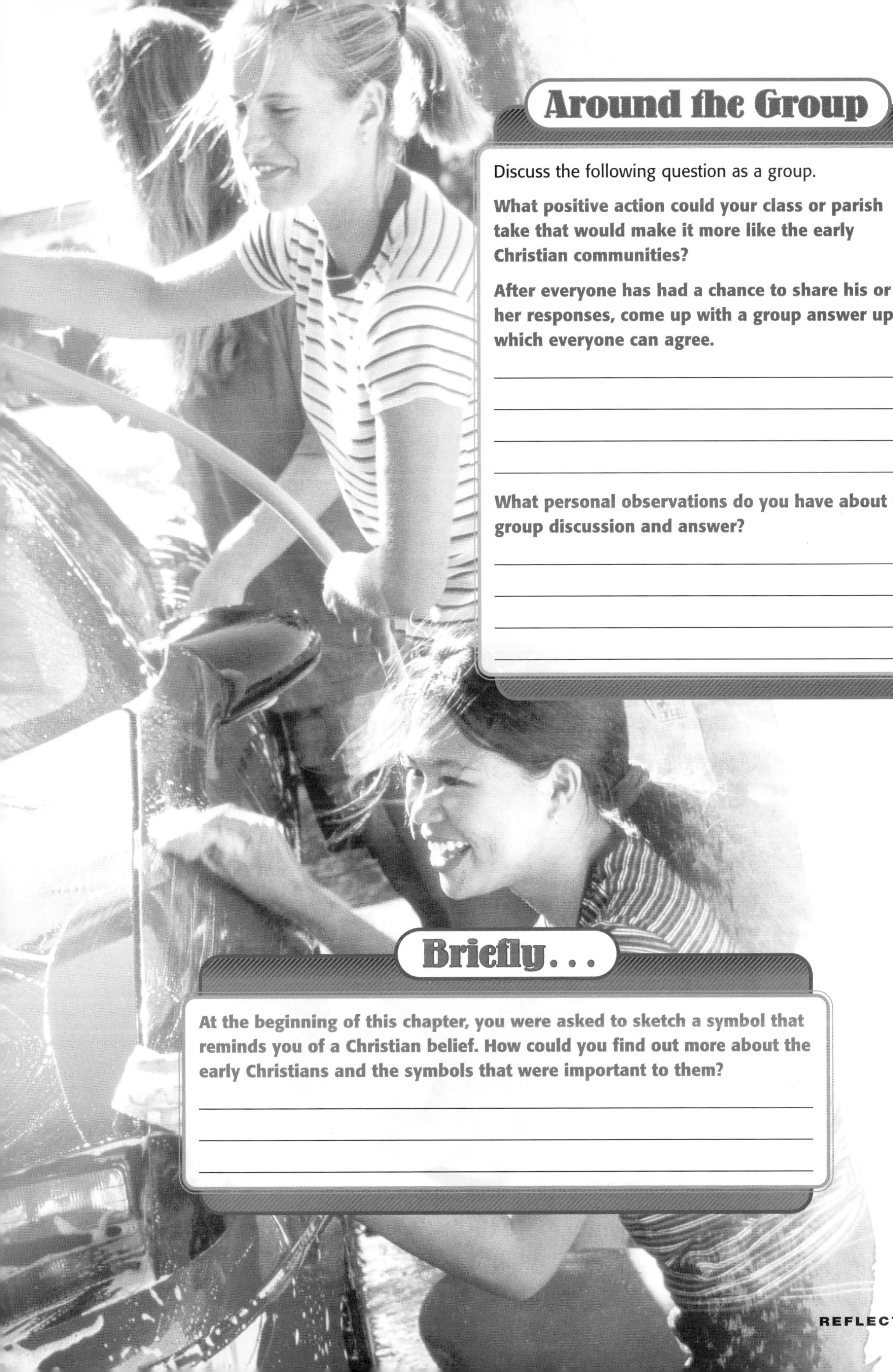

Around the Group

Discuss the following question as a group.

What positive action could your class or parish take that would make it more like the early Christian communities?

After everyone has had a chance to share his or her responses, come up with a group answer upon which everyone can agree.

_____

_____

_____

_____

What personal observations do you have about the group discussion and answer?

_____

_____

_____

_____

Briefly...

At the beginning of this chapter, you were asked to sketch a symbol that reminds you of a Christian belief. How could you find out more about the early Christians and the symbols that were important to them?

_____

_____

_____

Reconciling

Expressions of Faith—

The early Christians had to find ways to solve problems and forgive one another, and so do we. At the heart of our Christian story is the story of God's love and generosity. Jesus showed us how to forgive and how to seek forgiveness. Just as the early Christians found ways to forgive one another, we are called to forgive and reconcile with others.

Scripture

Bear with one another and, if anyone has a complaint against another, forgive each other; just as the Lord has forgiven you, so you also must forgive.

Colossians 3:13 Sunday After Christmas

Think About It—

You've probably needed forgiveness and reconciliation at some point in your life. You may have felt the pain of being separated from another person or of being hurt by something another person has said or done. Think about the times when you have experienced a need to forgive or be forgiven.

Circle the three words or phrases below that seem most related to forgiveness.

work it out   apologize   love

                                        give in

make it right   confess

                                        make excuses

forget   make up   start over

Skill Steps

The letters on Jesus' cross, INRI, meaning "Jesus of Nazareth, King of the Jews," can give us a method for seeking reconciliation.

Identify the wrong that was done and the trust that was broken.

No excuses should be made for what happened.

Responsible action is called for.

Identify a goal for strengthening the relationship.

Read the situations provided, and write one reason reconciliation did not happen. For each situation, suggest an action that might lead to a different result.

Maureen hurt her mother's feelings. She apologizes but then says, "I wouldn't be mad at you if you let me do what I want more often." The bad feelings remain.

Suggested action: _____

_____

_____

Chris and Matt had an argument. When Matt approaches Chris to apologize, Chris says, "I'm really mad at you, but I'll forgive you if you do whatever I want for a week."

Suggested action: _____

_____

_____

Check It Out

Share with your Faith Partner your responses from *Skill Steps*.

Place a check mark next to the sentences that apply to you.

○ People who know me say that I'm quick to forgive.

○ Even if I didn't cause the problem, I usually try to make up with the other person.

○ I find it easy to ask for forgiveness when I am at fault.

○ I try not to make excuses when I've done something wrong.

○ I've had a lot of good experiences of reconciling in the past.

Based on your responses, what kinds of things do you need to work on?

_____

_____

Closing Prayer

Holy Spirit, thank you for *guiding* the early Christians to *follow* Jesus and to *love* and **forgive** one another. Help us be willing to forgive and *reconcile.* Give us **courage** to reach out and seek *reconciliation* in our lives. Amen.

Forming
Community

Jesus, remember your Church here on earth. Be with our Church leaders as you were with your apostles, guiding and teaching them. Encourage us to share our gifts for the good of the Church and the world.

Circle the five actions you think are most important for someone trying to live his or her faith.

giving money to missions
praying
listening to others
improving grades
reading the Bible
practicing a sport
helping others
achieving success
showing kindness

going to Mass
obeying parents
being generous
watching the news
reading the paper
asking questions
forgiving
working for justice

Choose one of the actions that you do. Explain why it is important in your faith life and how you practice it.

_____

_____

_____

Living Our Faith

Is faith a set of beliefs we have, or is it the way we live? Our beliefs and our behavior are both important because

an active faith calls us to live what we believe. Our actions often show our beliefs more clearly than our words do. Qualities such as joy, compassion, generosity, and honesty are all important in our lives as Christians. As we imitate the actions of faithful people who demonstrate these qualities, we can grow to a point where our everyday lives naturally show what we believe.

The Command to Love

Jesus' command that we love one another as he has loved us is central to our Christian story. (See *John 15:12.*) This command is the basis for the community formed by Jesus. Within twenty years of Jesus' death and resurrection, the Church included many communities from Palestine to Rome.

The idea of worshiping one God seems natural to us, but the early Christians lived in a time when that was considered a strange idea by many people. The people of the Roman Empire worshiped many different gods and goddesses. In the temples of those religions, people offered sacrifices and held banquets. They tried to do what pleased the gods and goddesses, but they were never sure whether the gods and goddesses would treat them well or cause them harm.

Christians were different from the members of other religions in several ways. From the beginning the Christians gathered to hear and reflect on Scripture, which is the **word of God,** God's revelation of himself. Praising and thanking God the Father, they celebrated the **Eucharist,** in which the bread and wine were changed into the Body and Blood of Jesus, the Son of God.

Christianity offered something else that was very different from the religion of the Roman Empire—a loving God. From the beginning Christianity has taught that God loved the world so much that he sent us his only Son. God calls all humans to love him and to show this love by loving one another.

Catholics Believe

It is through the Spirit that the Church is made holy. See Catechism, #749.

In the space below, sketch one action of the Church that points to its holiness.

Heroes of
Our Faith

We can learn something about the first Christians from the books of the **New Testament,** the second part of the Bible. The New Testament includes the four Gospel accounts of Jesus, the Acts of the Apostles, some letters, and the Book of Revelation. Two men stand out from this period of the Church's story—Peter and Paul. Although these men were very different from each other, they both loved God and spread the **gospel** so that others would come to know the good news of God's saving love. Peter and Paul did not always agree with each other. When Peter first arrived in Antioch, a city in Turkey, he ate with both Jews and Gentiles. When other Jewish Christians began arriving from Jerusalem, they criticized Peter's practice of eating with Gentiles, and he stopped doing that. Paul took a stand against Peter's response, making it clear that Peter was not living what he claimed to believe—that Gentiles did not have to become Jews to be welcome in the Christian community. (See *Galatians 2:11–21*.)

OUR CHRISTIAN JOURNEY

First missionary journey, A.D. 46-48
Second missionary journey, A.D. 49-52
Third missionary journey, A.D. 53-57
Fourth missionary journey, A.D. 59-62

Spreading the Word Saul of Tarsus was born in Asia Minor (present-day Turkey). As a young Jew Paul believed that Christians were enemies of God and worked to have them arrested and imprisoned. After his conversion he traveled widely to spread the good news of God's kingdom and to establish and encourage communities of Jesus' followers. During his first missionary journey, Paul preached in Syria and Asia Minor. His second journey took him to Greece. During his third missionary journey, he returned to Greece but also visited Ephesus and other cities in Asia Minor.

In his letters Paul wrote of his own struggles and accomplishments, always connecting the meaning of his life and work to Jesus' life, suffering, death, and resurrection. His thoughts remain important to us today and form the basis of many later Christian teachings. Paul was eventually arrested and executed in Rome.

For further information: Learn more about Paul and his journeys by reading *Acts 15:36–28:31.*

1	100

c.5-c.65
PAUL'S LIFE

49
COUNCIL OF JERUSALEM

66-67
JEWISH REVOLT AGAINST ROME

70
JERUSALEM TEMPLE DESTROYED

Early Christian Prayer

We don't know much about the early Christian communities of faith. However, some of the writers of the New Testament included parts of early Christian hymns and prayers when they wrote their books and letters. For example, *Philippians 2:6–11* is part of a hymn sung centuries ago. The beauty of these verses gives us a glimpse of the poetry used in early Christian prayer, a beauty that is present in many of our prayers and hymns today.

Peter was one of the twelve apostles who gave up everything to follow Jesus. The Gospels of the New Testament tell us that Jesus appointed him to be the leader of the early disciples. Peter was quick to act, and he often did things that he regretted later. When Jesus had been arrested and was being questioned, Peter denied even knowing him. (See *Mark 14:66–72.*) But after Jesus' resurrection Peter was reconciled with Jesus through an experience in which Jesus told him, "Feed my lambs. . . . Tend my sheep" *(John 21:15–19).* Later Peter, through the power of the Holy Spirit, boldly preached, baptized, and healed in Jesus' name. He was among the first to spread the faith to Gentiles.

As a leader in the early Church, Peter led the Council of Jerusalem. He eventually went to Rome to preach the gospel. He was killed in Rome about A.D. 64 because of his faith in Jesus Christ and his efforts to spread the gospel.

Paul—also known by his Jewish name, Saul—had never met Jesus. As a young man he had worked against Christians before he became one. His turning point came as he traveled to Damascus to arrest followers of Jesus. Suddenly, a light from the sky flashed all around him, and he fell to the ground,

unable to see. He heard a voice asking, "Saul, Saul, why do you persecute me?" It was Jesus' voice, and his words changed Saul's life. (See *Acts 9:1–9.*) Eventually, Saul's sight was restored, and he began to see life from Jesus' viewpoint. From then on Paul confidently preached and acted in Jesus' name.

Paul traveled extensively, preaching the good news and starting Christian communities. Through those visits and his many letters, he continued to teach the communities about Jesus and advised them about specific problems they had as they tried to live as Christians. The Letter of Paul to the Romans, found in the New Testament, is one of the most complete statements of Paul's faith.

Sometimes when Paul wrote, he addressed his listeners using the Greek word *ekklesia,* which means "assembly." In 1 Timothy, Paul also gives us the first use of the terms *episkopos* (bishop) and *presbyteros* (priest). Paul was often arrested for teaching about Jesus. Many of his letters to early Christian communities were written from prison, where he must have spent hours pouring out his love and encouragement to the people scattered around the Roman Empire. Paul eventually went to Rome and was put to death there because he was a Christian.

Work with your Faith Partner to design a poster contrasting the lives of Peter and Paul.

FaiTH PaRTNeRSHiP

They not only cared for those who were poor in their own communities but also collected money for those who were in need in other communities. Some people outside their communities admired the way Christians showed their faith and hope, even in difficult times. Christians were known for the way they loved one another.

The **Church** today is still the community of believers who gather to hear the word of God and are nourished with the Eucharist. We are also called as the Body of Christ to show our love by serving one another. Be aware of how God might be calling you to respond to someone else's needs in the coming week.

Serving One
Another

Christians today come from a variety of backgrounds, and the New Testament tells us that the first Christians did also. Some were wealthy; some were poor. Some were free; others were slaves. Early Christians also came from many occupations. Paul, Aquila, and Priscilla were tentmakers by trade. Lydia sold purple cloth, an expensive item because it was so difficult to make purple dye. Erastus was the city treasurer of Corinth, Manaen was a member of Herod's court, and Cornelius was a Roman commander. Each one had gifts to contribute to his or her community, just as we do.

The Christians followed Jesus' example of being a servant to all. Everyone contributed to the community. Those who had little money gave their time to care for others. They comforted one another in times of trouble.

Opening the Word

2nd Sunday of Easter, Cycle B

Now the whole group of those who believed were of one heart and soul, and no one claimed private ownership of any possessions, but everything they owned was held in common. Acts 4:32

Read *Acts 4:32–34* as well as *Acts 2:44–47* and *1 Corinthians 16:13–24.* How were the early Christians taught to live as communities of faith? What does this mean for us today?

_____

_____

_____

Share with your Faith Partner your thoughts about how we can live as a community of faith.

Life in the **Spirit**

The early Christians showed their love for God by looking out for and taking care of one another. They freely and generously contributed their gifts and possessions to build up the community.

As Catholics we are called to do the same. Through Baptism we become members of the Church. The Holy Spirit acts in our lives to draw us closer to God and continually invites us to open our hearts. With other believers we pray, celebrate the Eucharist, and hear the word of God, just as the early Christians did. We support and care for one another through our words and actions.

Our lives are connected to the lives of others. Once we understand this, we realize that we are called to act as Jesus did, helping those people who are poor or suffering, those who have no power to help themselves, and those who are being threatened or harmed by others. By working at a local food bank, collecting used clothing, or working with others to improve someone's living conditions, you can use your gifts to share God's love and help build up the community.

The Holy Spirit gave the early Christians the strength and generosity to help those who were most in need. The Spirit offers us the same gifts and challenges. Membership in the Christian community calls us to use our gifts to serve others.

Reflect on what membership in the Christian community calls you to be and do. Share your thoughts with your Faith Partner.

FaiTH PaRTNeRSHiP

WRAP UP

- •Jesus' command to love one another called the early Christians to form communities and share the gospel with others.
- •The unique gifts of Peter and Paul helped establish and guide early Christian communities.
- •The early Christians gathered to hear the word of God, celebrate the Eucharist, and take care of one another.

What questions do you have about the content of this chapter?

_____

_____

_____

Around the Group

Discuss the following question as a group.

What are some characteristics of the first Christian communities that you think are still evident in the life of the Church?

After everyone has had a chance to share his or her responses, come up with a group answer upon which everyone can agree.

_____

_____

_____

_____

What personal observations do you have about the group discussion and answer?

_____

_____

_____

_____

Briefly...

At the beginning of this chapter, you were asked to consider the importance of certain actions in living your faith. How can participating in a faith community help you live your faith today?

_____

_____

_____

Reconciling

Expressions of Faith-

The members of the early Church were encouraged to work through their problems toward the unity of the Body of Christ. Each day we have many opportunities to apply that same reconciling spirit in our own lives.

Scripture

"So when you are offering your gift at the altar, if you remember that your brother or sister has something against you, leave your gift there before the altar and go; first be reconciled to your brother or sister, and then come and offer your gift."

Matthew 5:23–24 6th Sunday in Ordinary Time, Cycle A

Skill Steps-

Recall how we can reconcile with someone when there has been a disagreement or some other painful separation. As you practice this skill, here are some key points to remember:

● At the heart of our Christian story is the belief that Jesus' suffering, death, and resurrection reconciled us with God.

● INRI can remind us of Jesus' sacrifice and of how we can practice reconciling.

● Reconciling is a form of peacemaking.

● Reconciliation strengthens a relationship for the future.

Identify the wrong that was done and the trust that was broken.

No excuses should be made for what happened.

Responsible action is called for.

Identify a goal for strengthening the relationship.

Skill Builder-

Look at the following situations and decide how INRI can be used in each.

○ You borrowed your brother's favorite CD without telling him and then lost it on the bus during a field trip.

_____

_____

○ Someone made fun of your uncle because he is Jewish, and you laughed along.

_____

_____

Putting It into Practice-

Think about your life, and identify one situation in which forgiveness and reconciliation are needed. Tell how you would apply the INRI method in this situation.

I- Identify the wrong: Name the problem as you see it.

_____

_____

N- No excuses: Don't try to excuse or rationalize your part in what happened. Accept your role in the problem, and go from there.

_____

_____

R- Responsible action: What will you do to forgive or to bring about reconciliation and rebuild trust?

_____

_____

I- Identify the goal: What kind of relationship do you want with the other person, and how can you encourage that?

_____

_____

Each time you find yourself in a situation that calls for forgiveness and reconciliation, use INRI to help you see what can be done.

Review the INRI steps, and list one part of the skill that you are good at and one that you need to work on.

_____

_____

_____

Closing Prayer-

Thank you, God, for the gifts that the early Church passed on to us. We know you are the one who makes a caring community possible. Help us include others in our circle of caring. Amen.

CHAPTER 3

Witnessing to the World

Lord, you know that we face many pressures. Sometimes it seems that everyone wants something different from us. Help us trust that you care for us. Give us the wisdom and courage we need to share our faith in you.

List or sketch in the space provided some of the pressures you face in your life.

What are some things you do to handle these pressures?

_____

_____

What could help you handle pressure better?

_____

_____

Coping with Pressures

We face pressure every day. Some pressure is useful because it reminds us to be responsible. It challenges us to use our strengths in the best way possible. Our friends can pressure us to do what is right and develop our talents. This is positive peer pressure.

On the other hand, our friends can pressure us to make poor choices, even choices that are morally wrong. Such negative peer pressure includes pressure to smoke, drink, use drugs, experiment with sex, vandalize, or steal. These pressures force us to decide whether or not we can live our faith. We are better able to ignore or resist negative pressures when, through God's grace, we are confident about who we are and what we believe.

The Holy Spirit can give you the courage to recognize and deal with these pressures, just as the Spirit was with the Church even when the early Christians were being mocked and punished for their beliefs.

Christians Under Suspicion

Saint Polycarp

OUR CHRISTIAN JOURNEY

The Faithfulness of the Martyrs

Vibia Perpetua, a young woman of noble birth, lived in Carthage, a city in North Africa. She and her slave Felicity were catechumens, and their catechist, Saturus, was preparing them for Baptism. They were all arrested and taken to prison, even though Perpetua had a small infant and Felicity was pregnant. The young women would not deny their faith to escape persecution. In A.D. 203, three days before they were to be executed, Felicity gave birth. When the time came for their deaths, Perpetua, Felicity, and their companions were all flogged and led into the amphitheater, where they were killed. The story of Perpetua and Felicity is important because they represent the courage and goodness associated with many of the martyrs. The feast day for Saints Perpetua and Felicity is March 7.

For further information: Use a Catholic encyclopedia or a book of the saints to learn more about martyrs in the early Church.

Have you ever been wrongly accused of doing something that harmed other people or their property? The early Christians often found themselves in that situation. Many Romans knew very little about the small, scattered Christian communities. There were rumors about the "body" and "blood" of the Eucharist, and some people thought that the Christians were cannibals. Others noticed that Jesus' followers believed in the equality of all people and refused to worship the gods of Rome. This convinced many people that Christians wanted to overthrow the government. For these reasons many people were suspicious of Christianity. In the first century the Roman Emperor Nero blamed Christians for setting a fire that burned down much of the city of Rome.

As we have already learned, our Christian story began and grew in the cities, towns, and villages of the Roman Empire. The Roman army patrolled the empire, keeping the peace. This system maintained law and brought order to the area around the Mediterranean Sea, parts of Europe, and as far north as present-day Britain and Ireland.

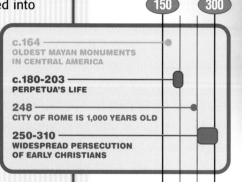

150   300

c.164
OLDEST MAYAN MONUMENTS
IN CENTRAL AMERICA

c.180-203
PERPETUA'S LIFE

248
CITY OF ROME IS 1,000 YEARS OLD

250-310
WIDESPREAD PERSECUTION
OF EARLY CHRISTIANS

Saint Stephen

By about a hundred years after Jesus' death and resurrection, his followers had traveled extensively in the Roman Empire to establish Christian communities. These **missionaries** carried the good news of God's kingdom to people and cultures different from their own. However, by A.D. 150, Christians were still relatively few in number, and Roman officials did not consider them important in the life of the empire.

The farther from Rome the empire grew, the harder it became to manage. There were many peaceful people in the empire, but there were also many warlike groups. Most people believed that political power was a gift of the gods and that an emperor could rule successfully only if the gods supported him. Since the Romans were the conquerors, their gods were considered the strongest. When conditions in the empire deteriorated, the emperors decided that they would require people to show their loyalty to Rome by offering sacrifices to the Roman gods.

Saint Agnes

Christians refused to offer sacrifice to the Roman gods. Eventually, the Roman Empire began to see Christians as irreligious trouble-makers who interfered with the government's need to keep things under control.

Persecution

From the beginning Christians felt pressure from many directions. Tensions between Gentiles and Jews led to a dispute that resulted in the death of Stephen, a Christian known for his holiness and good works. Led by the Spirit, Stephen spoke with wisdom and performed great wonders among the people. He was arrested and brought before the Jewish council, and false witnesses spoke against him. Stephen argued that Jesus was the Messiah who had been foretold and that these Jewish people had rejected Jesus. His speech angered the crowd, and they dragged Stephen out of the city and stoned him to death. Those who stoned Stephen laid their cloaks at the feet of the young man Saul. Stephen is the Church's first **martyr,** one who witnessed to Christ and was killed for being a follower of Jesus.

Catholics Believe

Martyrdom means courageously bearing witness to the truth of the faith, even when you are facing death. See Catechism, #2473.

What belief or value is so important to you that you would be willing to die for it?

_____

_____

_____

Discuss your thoughts with your Faith Partner.

FaiTH PaRTNeRSHiP

But even if you do suffer for doing what is right, you are blessed. Do not fear what they fear, and do not be intimidated, but in your hearts sanctify Christ as Lord. 1 Peter 3:14–15

Read *1 Peter 3:13–18* as well as *Philippians 1:27–30, 1 Timothy 6:11–12,* and *2 Timothy 1:1–7.* Sketch a symbol or an action that shows the faith and courage that these passages indicate Christians need to have.

In Ephesus, in what is now Turkey, silversmiths were accustomed to making and selling statues of Artemis, goddess of the hunt. When Paul began preaching in that area, the silversmiths were afraid that the gospel message would hurt their business. Paul told people about the living God and taught that gods made with human hands are not gods. The angry silversmiths started a riot and blamed it on the Christians.

The tendency to blame Christians continued into the second and third centuries, as the empire experienced trouble maintaining its control and protecting its citizens. Roman officials believed that having public executions would help maintain law and order by showing what happened to people who caused problems. Sometimes criminals were thrown to lions or other wild beasts. Many Christians were unfairly accused and were also killed in this way. The Christian thinker Tertullian observed that anytime there was a riot or the threat of a mob going wild, someone would cry out, "Christians to the lions!"

This period of **persecution** of Christians lasted about three hundred years, with the worst time of persecution being between A.D. 250 and 310. (The persecution was not continual and did not take place everywhere.) The faith of martyrs gave other Christians the courage to die for Christ. They died for Christ, just as he had died for them. Today we consider many martyrs also to be **saints,** people whose lives exemplify holiness and dedication to God.

ROME
ANTIOCH
Mediterranean Sea
Alexandria

Our Global Community

Praying for Freedom

Some governments try to stop the spread of any religion that might threaten their power. The conflicts can result in persecution, torture, and death. Christians are being persecuted in many areas of our world, including parts of China, India, the Middle East, Africa, Mexico, and Central America. In some places Christian leaders are imprisoned and churches are burned down. We can pray that people around the world will be free to live their faith without fear of persecution.

The Church Grows

By the fourth century the Church was growing throughout the empire. The persecutions that were intended to stop the spread of Christianity actually encouraged it. Other Christians grew stronger in their own faith when they saw the courage and holiness shown by the martyrs. In time the tombs of martyrs buried in the catacombs of Rome became Christian shrines. Missionaries spread the faith, and they visited and wrote letters of encouragement to the communities they had established. In the meantime, the empire itself had become so big that it was divided into a western half and an eastern half, with co-emperors ruling the two parts.

Rome was still the capital of the empire, and over time it had become the most important center of Christianity in the western part of the Roman Empire. Christians began to turn to the bishop of Rome to settle disputes and protect the rights of the other bishops.

Alexandria, Egypt, was the second most important center of Christianity. There was a well-known Christian school of thought in Alexandria, and the Christian community in that city was respected for its wisdom, which was shown by people such as Clement, Origen, and Catherine.

Antioch also remained an important center of Christianity during this time. Many courageous Christians such as Ignatius, a bishop in Antioch, were martyred in that city for their faith.

Early followers of Jesus were sometimes pressured to give up their faith. They were looked down upon and mocked, and they were refused jobs and good housing. To endure such hardships, they needed a strong sense of who and what they believed in, as well as the support and strength of the community.

Think about how you would feel if someone from your parish or school community were killed because he or she was a Christian. Share your thoughts with your Faith Partner.

FaiTH PaRTNeRSHiP

Witnessing Through Our Actions

Most of us will probably not have to face the life-threatening persecution that the early Christians endured. But we may face others' criticism or disapproval when we participate in a project that shows respect for life, such as a Right to Life march or a protest against the death penalty. Our own courageous, moral action may challenge our critics to actions they need to take. Some people may be angry with us for trying to change the way things are done. But our actions witness to God's love for all his children.

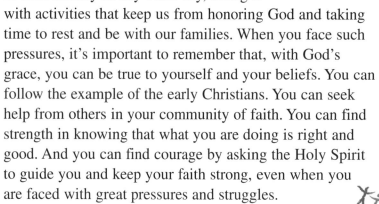

As Christians we may feel pressure to treat Sunday as any other day, filling it with activities that keep us from honoring God and taking time to rest and be with our families. When you face such pressures, it's important to remember that, with God's grace, you can be true to yourself and your beliefs. You can follow the example of the early Christians. You can seek help from others in your community of faith. You can find strength in knowing that what you are doing is right and good. And you can find courage by asking the Holy Spirit to guide you and keep your faith strong, even when you are faced with great pressures and struggles.

Reflect on how you can witness to Christ and to God's love. Share your thoughts with your Faith Partner.

FaiTH PaRTNeRSHiP

WRAP UP

- •Christianity had spread to many parts of the Roman Empire within a century or so of Jesus' death and resurrection.
- •The early Christians were persecuted, and some were martyred for their faith.
- •Many martyrs are also declared saints because they give us an example of holiness.
- •Many Christians show courage when they are being persecuted.

What questions do you have about the content of this chapter?

_____

_____

_____

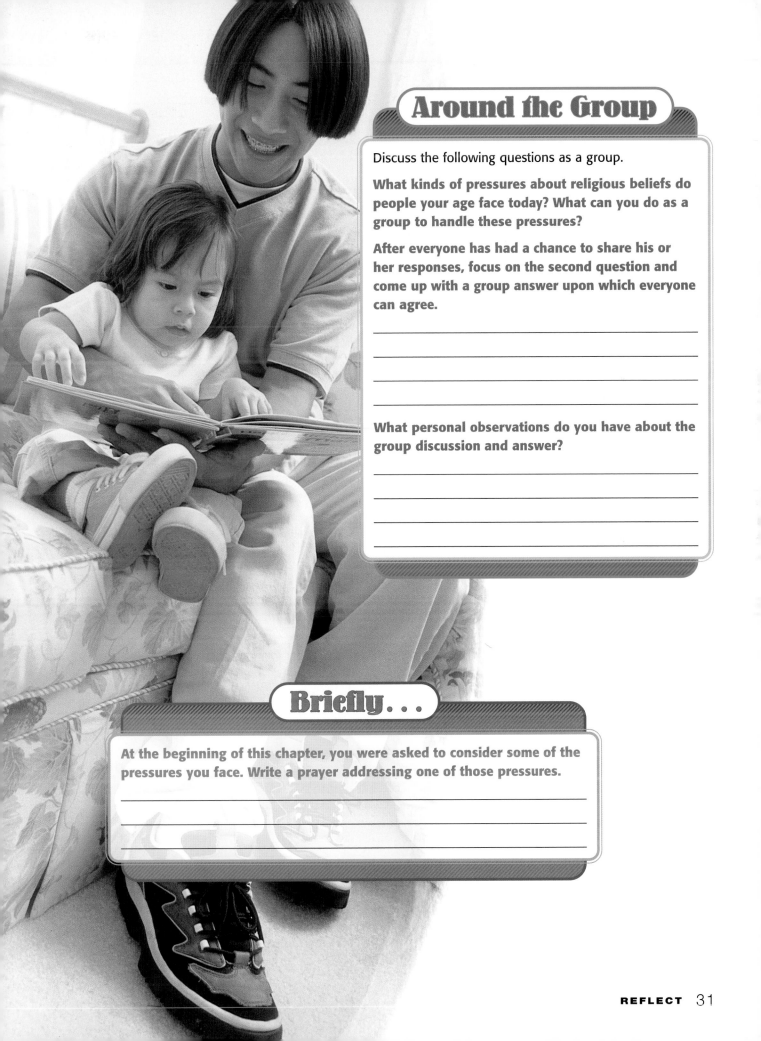

Around the Group

Discuss the following questions as a group.

What kinds of pressures about religious beliefs do people your age face today? What can you do as a group to handle these pressures?

After everyone has had a chance to share his or her responses, focus on the second question and come up with a group answer upon which everyone can agree.

_____
_____
_____

What personal observations do you have about the group discussion and answer?

_____
_____
_____
_____

Briefly...

At the beginning of this chapter, you were asked to consider some of the pressures you face. Write a prayer addressing one of those pressures.

_____
_____
_____

Handling Anger

Expressions of Faith—

The early Christians had many reasons to be angry with the Romans. Instead, these Christians showed the virtue of temperance by not arguing or fighting with those who were persecuting them. They gave witness to living in peace. Learning how to handle your anger is a key Skill for Christian living.

Think About It—

Everyone experiences anger at some point in life. People react differently when they are angry. Some are slow to anger and quick to forgive. Others get angry quickly or hold grudges. Some people forget what they were angry about very soon after they have expressed themselves. Describe your own experiences of anger below:

⚪ A time recently when I have been angry:

_____

_____

_____

⚪ An example of a time when I handled anger well:

_____

_____

_____

⚪ Complete this sentence: The best way to handle anger is

_____

_____

_____

Skill Steps-

One good way to handle any strong emotion you might experience is to Name It, Tame It, and Claim It. When dealing with your anger, you have the responsibility to keep it under control. You may find it helpful to follow these steps.

- Naming all the emotions you feel helps you recognize what you are experiencing. Sometimes when you think you're angry, you may actually be feeling embarrassed or rejected. Spend some time in quiet to reflect on exactly what you are feeling.
- Gain some control over your anger by taming it rather than letting it control you. Recognize inappropriate and morally wrong responses, such as physical violence, cruel words, cursing, refusal to talk, road rage, and use of weapons. When you feel angry, take time to wonder and wait. *Wonder* whether or not you have all the facts. Wonder if the person meant his or her remark the way you took it. Wonder if you are making too much of the situation. Then *wait* before you say or do anything. Give yourself time to get through the rush of anger. Distract yourself by doing something else. Leave the room. Count to twenty. Take a walk. Listen to a favorite song. Pray for God's guidance to help you see a bigger picture.
- Claiming the emotion means putting it to good use. If you're angry, don't act on it. Let your anger motivate you to do what is right. Realize the importance of expressing your feelings in an appropriate manner.

Check It Out-

Rate yourself on a scale of 1 to 5, with 1 being "almost always" and 5 being "almost never."

	1	2	3	4	5
I don't get angry.	○	○	○	○	○
I get angry, but I control it well.	○	○	○	○	○
I try not to hurt people when I get angry.	○	○	○	○	○
I am self-disciplined.	○	○	○	○	○
I use my anger as a reminder to think before I act.	○	○	○	○	○
I express my feelings in appropriate ways.	○	○	○	○	○

Based on how you rated yourself, what do you need to work on to become better at handling anger?

_____

_____

Closing Prayer-

O Holy Spirit, help us stand up for what is right. Give us the wisdom and courage to share the good news of the gospel with others. Help us see how we can be strong in our faith yet respectful of others' religious beliefs. Amen.

The Christian Church Grows

Praise to you, heavenly Father, Creator of the universe. Praise to you, Jesus, Son of God, Redeemer. Praise to you, Holy Spirit, Sanctifier, Counselor who guides us. Praise to the triune God, three in one, who cares for us without end.

On a scale of 1 to 5, with 1 being "always" and 5 being "never," indicate how often you recognize signs of God's presence in your daily life?

	1	2	3	4	5
When I'm out in nature	○	○	○	○	○
When I read the Bible	○	○	○	○	○
When I'm with family members	○	○	○	○	○
When I go to church	○	○	○	○	○
When I'm with other people	○	○	○	○	○
In happy moments	○	○	○	○	○
In times of trouble	○	○	○	○	○

Name another time, place, or activity that makes you aware of God's presence.

_____

_____

_____

God with Us

Each day we have experiences that can remind us of God's presence in our lives. When we notice all the goodness of God in our lives, we often feel thankful and our faith in him grows. We begin to understand that we can depend on God to be with us in any kind of situation.

The first Christians loved God, even though their faithfulness led to persecution. It was hard for them to live their faith—but they did, trusting that God was always with them. Once Christians were allowed to live their faith openly, the Church spread into new areas of the Roman Empire. The freedom to live their faith enabled Christians to express their love for God in marvelous ways.

Freedom to **Believe**

We are free to decide how, when, and where we worship God. The first Christians were not. But an important decision early in the fourth century made Christianity a tolerated religion in the Roman Empire. Constantine, the emperor in the West, was convinced that the God of the Christians had helped him and his troops win the victory that enabled him to rise to power. In conjunction with Licinius, the emperor in the East, Constantine granted Christianity and all other religions official tolerance.

In 330 Constantine moved the capital of the Roman Empire from Rome to Constantinople, a city he named after himself. Fifty years later Emperor Theodosius made Christianity the official religion of the Roman Empire (380) and forbade the worship of other gods (392).

Because of its size and the diverse groups of people that lived within it, the Roman Empire was difficult to manage well. The western and eastern parts were beginning to be very different from each other.

The Church in the East and the Church in the West each began to take on their own unique character. Because of its long history, Rome never lost its influence. Over time both Rome and Constantinople developed as important centers, and eventually the empire split, with the Roman Empire in the West and the Byzantine Empire in the East.

Opening the Word

5th Sunday of Easter, Cycle C

"I give you a new commandment, that you love one another. Just as I have loved you, you also should love one another." John 13:34

Read *John 13:31–35* as well as *Matthew 5:14–16, 7:1–5* and *Ephesians 5:15–20.* How are we to conduct our lives in the Christian spirit?

_____

_____

_____

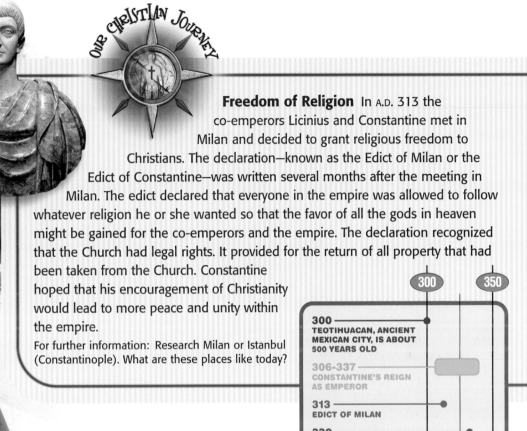

Freedom of Religion In A.D. 313 the co-emperors Licinius and Constantine met in Milan and decided to grant religious freedom to Christians. The declaration—known as the Edict of Milan or the Edict of Constantine—was written several months after the meeting in Milan. The edict declared that everyone in the empire was allowed to follow whatever religion he or she wanted so that the favor of all the gods in heaven might be gained for the co-emperors and the empire. The declaration recognized that the Church had legal rights. It provided for the return of all property that had been taken from the Church. Constantine hoped that his encouragement of Christianity would lead to more peace and unity within the empire.

For further information: Research Milan or Istanbul (Constantinople). What are these places like today?

300 | 350

300
TEOTIHUACAN, ANCIENT MEXICAN CITY, IS ABOUT 500 YEARS OLD

306-337
CONSTANTINE'S REIGN AS EMPEROR

313
EDICT OF MILAN

330
CAPITAL OF THE ROMAN EMPIRE MOVED TO CONSTANTINOPLE

East and West

In the eastern part of the empire, the Church entered a period of great creativity. Beautiful hymns and prayers were written. Vestments and chalices as well as mosaics and church buildings were designed to give glory to God. Theology, the study of God, took on more importance. Following the practice of the early Church, the bishop of Constantinople allowed the people to pray and worship in their own languages.

In the western part of the empire, with Rome as its center, the Church experienced tremendous growth. The Germanic peoples were conquered and brought into the empire and the Church.

About 460 Patrick took the message of Christianity to the Celtic people of Ireland. As a young boy Patrick had been captured and taken to Ireland as a slave. As a young adult he escaped and was reunited with his family.

A few years later Patrick returned to Ireland to evangelize—to teach and preach the good news. Patrick's work of **evangelization** in Ireland flourished, and many people there became Christians.

In 410 the city of Rome was taken by force by a Germanic tribe. The government could no longer function, so the most important person left in Rome was its bishop. The bishop of Rome was now called the pope and led other churches in the empire. Citizens of the western part of the Roman Empire also looked up to him as their political leader.

Rome and Constantinople became the two main centers of Christianity. Islam, a religion begun by the prophet Muhammad (A.D. 570–632) in Arabia, began to spread throughout the Mediterranean world. As Islam became more important in the East, Christianity slowly grew stronger in the West.

Leading the **Faithful**

In the West the Church's structure began to look more and more like the structure of the Roman Empire. For example, what was originally a region of the empire became a diocese, the region under the responsibility of a Church leader called a bishop. In a process that began with Jesus' appointing of the apostles, bishops of every age have been and are given the authority to lead the Church. Through this **apostolic succession,** the Church has been and will continue to be taught, sanctified, and guided. Priests and deacons were ordained to help the bishops guide the Church.

Because of this system of organization, Christians—most of whom were uneducated—could depend on their bishops, priests, and deacons to answer questions, solve problems, and give advice. In fact the Mass that was celebrated by Christians of this time was very similar to the one we know today. People heard the Scriptures read and explained to them as part of their worship. Gifts of bread and wine were brought, and a prayer of thanksgiving was prayed over them as they became the Body and Blood of Christ.

During the fourth century Jerome, a scholar and translator, translated Old Testament books from Hebrew into Latin. He also improved Latin translations of the books of what we call the New Testament.

His Latin translation of the Bible is called the *Vulgate,* from the Latin word meaning "in the common language of the people." The Vulgate became the official version of the Bible and was used by the Church for centuries.

By about the fourth century, Christians were openly discussing and debating their questions of faith. Two important Church councils, the Council of Nicaea and the Council of Chalcedon, helped answer questions about Christ being fully human and fully divine and about the Holy Spirit as a Person of the Trinity.

Focus On

Images of Holiness

Icons are pictures of saints or scenes from Scripture that are meant to show the holy qualities of God and the saints rather than to picture scenes and people realistically. The use of icons originated in the Church in the East, where they are still used in the devotions of Christians. Through the centuries many people have found that icons help them pray.

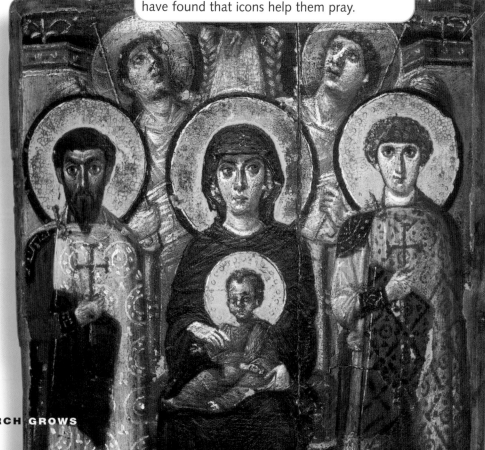

Church Fathers	Known For
Ambrose c. 340–397 West—Milan, Italy	Teaching about Christ being the Son of God
Athanasius c. 297–373 East—Alexandria, Egypt	Writing about faith and attending Church councils
Augustine 354–430 West—Hippo, North Africa	Writing about grace and the sacraments
Cyril of Alexandria c. 375–444 East—Alexandria, Egypt	Teaching that Mary is the Mother of God
Jerome c. 340–c. 420 West—Italy, Syria, Palestine	Translating the books of the Bible into Latin
John Chrysostom c. 347–407 East—Constantinople	Preaching brilliant sermons and writing many of the prayers used in the Divine Liturgy in the East

The Church's faith survived difficult times because the early Christians were clear about their beliefs. The **Apostles' Creed,** a summary of what the apostles had taught, explained the Christian faith in a way that most people could understand. This creed also explained that the Church was holy and **catholic,** which means that it is universal and is intended for everyone.

During this period the example of personal holiness shown by the **Church fathers** provided great encouragement for the Church. These faithful men shared their knowledge and wisdom to help Christians learn how to live their faith.

Throughout the history of the Church, one thing has remained the same: the Holy Spirit has continually guided Christians in using their gifts to strengthen the Church and to share the good news of the gospel with the rest of the world.

Catholics Believe

Christ pours out the Holy Spirit on the members of the Church to nourish, heal, and organize them according to their gifts.
See Catechism, #739.

How do you recognize the Holy Spirit at work in your life? Explain.

_____

_____

_____

Share your thoughts with your Faith Partner.

Understanding
Our Faith

Once the Church was tolerated in the Roman Empire, Christians could openly worship the Christian God. Although we may face family or peer pressure not to appear overly religious, we have the right to live our faith. Whatever our circumstances, we can live as followers of Christ.

When we come together to worship as a community, God shares himself with us through the words of Scripture and the Eucharist, and we gradually understand more about our faith as Christians. As we study the Church's story and its teachings, the Holy Spirit continues to help us grow in understanding. We discover how the saints and other Christians before us lived their faith. One of our primary tasks as Christians is to become more aware of the Holy Spirit's continuing action in our own lives and in the world. The Holy Spirit leads us to live our faith by sharing our gifts with others.

Our daily experiences with other people can lead us to a greater understanding of our faith. We begin to discover that both our prayers and our actions are important in a life of faith. When we reach out to help a friend or classmate who is facing a tough situation, or when someone reaches out to help us, we may discover the truth of Jesus' words, "Truly I tell you, just as you did it to one of the least of these who are members of my family, you did it to me" *(Matthew 25:40)*.

Reflect on who or what has helped you better understand your faith. Share your thoughts with your Faith Partner.

FAiTH PaRTNeRSHiP

WRAP UP

- **The emperor Constantine allowed Christians to live their faith openly.**
- **At various times in both the East and the West, the Church enjoyed periods of great growth and creativity.**
- **The Church councils and the Church fathers helped Christians better understand and express their faith.**
- **The Holy Spirit is always present to guide the Church.**

What questions do you have about the content of this chapter?

_____

_____

_____

Around the Group

Discuss the following question as a group.

If you had to explain Christianity to someone who had never heard of it, what would you say about it?

After everyone has had a chance to share his or her responses, come up with a group answer upon which everyone can agree.

_____

_____

_____

_____

What personal observations do you have about the group discussion and answer?

_____

_____

_____

_____

Briefly...

At the beginning of this chapter, you were asked to consider when and where you recognize God's presence. Explore that idea further by naming some of the people, words, images, and actions that help you understand your faith.

_____

_____

Handling Anger

Expressions of Faith-

Many early Christians used the "fuel" of their anger to show love and build up the community instead of acting in revenge. Some of the enemies of the Church noticed this loving response and also became Christians.

Skill Steps-

The message from *James 1:19-20* can remind us of the steps for handling anger—naming, taming, and claiming.

When we have a strong urge to express angry feelings, we can choose to listen before we speak and wait before we react. Realizing that we can choose our response helps us understand that we can control even a powerful emotion like anger.

Here are some things to remember as you practice this skill:

● Try to recognize and name whatever feelings you are experiencing.

● Anger is a normal emotion, but there are appropriate and inappropriate ways to respond when you are angry.

● When you become angry, you can seek the Holy Spirit's guidance in handling your anger.

Skill Builder-

Write an appropriate response and an inappropriate response for each of these situations involving anger.

○ Margo was angry that her father caught her lying about a test grade. As soon as her father spoke to her, Margo decided to

Appropriate response: _____

Inappropriate response: _____

○ Carl and Amanda were good friends, but one day they had an argument. Carl was hurt and angry. He decided to

Appropriate response: _____

Inappropriate response: _____

Putting It into Practice-

Think of a current situation about which you feel angry. Then complete the Name It, Tame It, Claim It process to help you in handling your anger.

Name It
○ The situation: _____
○ How I really feel when I think about it: _____
_____

Tame It
○ What I wonder about this situation: _____
_____

○ What I can do to practice waiting in this situation: _____
_____

Claim It
○ Something I have learned from this situation: _____
_____

○ Something about myself I have realized: _____
_____

○ What I can do to make positive use of this experience: _____
_____

You can avoid a fast, angry reaction by taking time to describe what you are feeling and reminding yourself to wonder and wait. Deciding what positive action you can take is a way to channel your anger.

_____

Now that you have had some practice in naming, taming, and claiming your anger, list below one aspect of handling anger that you are good at and one that you still need to work on.

_____
_____

Closing Prayer-

God of heaven and earth, thank you for our Christian story and the way it helps us see your love for us. You help us understand ourselves better. You challenge us to learn to handle our emotions. Help us control our anger and respond in appropriate ways. Amen.

CHAPTER 5

Church and Culture

Holy Spirit, you are the wisdom of all ages. You give us what we need to build up the Church and to share the good news of the gospel. Help us be generous and share with others all that you give us. Amen.

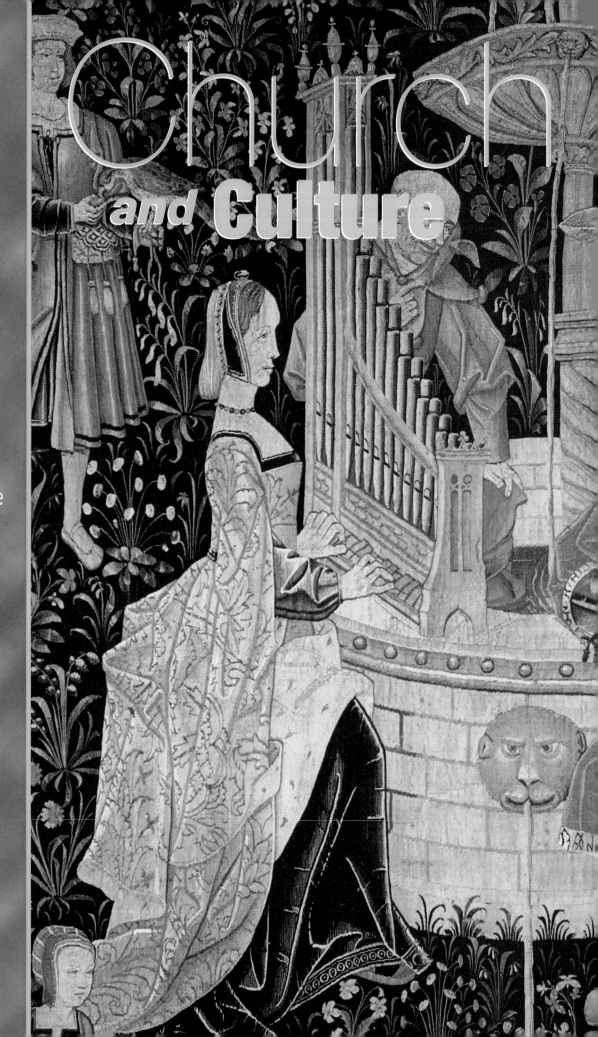

What Do You Think?

What gifts and abilities do you have? Circle the number that expresses how talented you think you are in each of the areas listed below.

	Very Talented		Somewhat		Not At All
Music	1	2	3	4	5
Sports	1	2	3	4	5
Writing	1	2	3	4	5
Math	1	2	3	4	5
Communicating	1	2	3	4	5
Science	1	2	3	4	5
Art	1	2	3	4	5

Which one of your talents is most important to you?

Using Our Gifts

All of us have God-given talents and abilities. We develop some of our talents through practice and hard work. Others seem to come naturally. As Christians we are called to share our talents and abilities so they may be used for the good of the community. When we use our talents in this way, our hearts open to new possibilities. Many people have discovered that when they use their gifts generously, they are especially blessed themselves. Which of the gifts mentioned above have you used generously? Which would you like to use more generously? What other gifts do you have that could be used to help others?

By using the talents and abilities God has given us, we contribute to the culture and society in which we live. Both as individuals and as part of the community of the Church, we have opportunities to respond to the needs of the world. Throughout its history the Church has played an important role in shaping the cultures in which Christians live.

Christianity in **Europe**

Imagine for a moment that every large city you know is a kingdom with its own ruler. This ruler has an army and controls all the smaller towns and the highways in the area. The setting for our Christian story after the fall of Rome in 476 was much like this. During the fifth century various Germanic tribes migrated south and west across the Roman Empire, and the countryside became a dangerous place. This situation continued until the reign of Charlemagne, a king remembered for uniting much of Europe.

Opening the Word

Pentecost

Now there are varieties of gifts, but the same Spirit; and there are varieties of services, but the same Lord; and there are varieties of activities, but it is the same God who activates all of them in everyone. 1 Corinthians 12:4–6

Read *1 Corinthians 12:4–12*, as well as *Mark 4:1–9, James 2:17,* and *1 Peter 4:9–11.* Sketch or describe in words a gift that you have seen a friend or family member sharing with the rest of the Church community.

Charlemagne became "Holy Roman Emperor" in 800, having formed an alliance with the bishop of Rome, Pope Leo III. Charlemagne promoted education through the copying of books and the building of schools. He also was one of the first rulers to give significant power to local bishops. Under Charlemagne's leadership, Europe began to think of itself as *Christendom,* an entirely Christian society, and the Church became the main civilizing force of the **Middle Ages,** the period of European history from about A.D. 500 to 1500.

As the towns and villages became unified under Charlemagne, *feudalism* began to develop. Under the system of feudalism, local peasants would give some of the grain and livestock they raised in exchange for protection provided by landowners, who were often called lords. Most government during the Middle Ages revolved around the feudal system.

Because of the power Charlemagne gave the Church, many bishops, especially the pope, became rulers in their own right, with lands to oversee and armies to protect them. But after Charlemagne's death in 814, the Holy Roman Empire began to lose power. After a brief power struggle, three of Charlemagne's grandsons divided the Empire. But the central control that their grandfather maintained was lost under the leadership of his grandsons, and the Church was left as the only established and unifying force throughout Europe. With the Church as its guide, the Middle Ages became a time of great artistic and intellectual achievement.

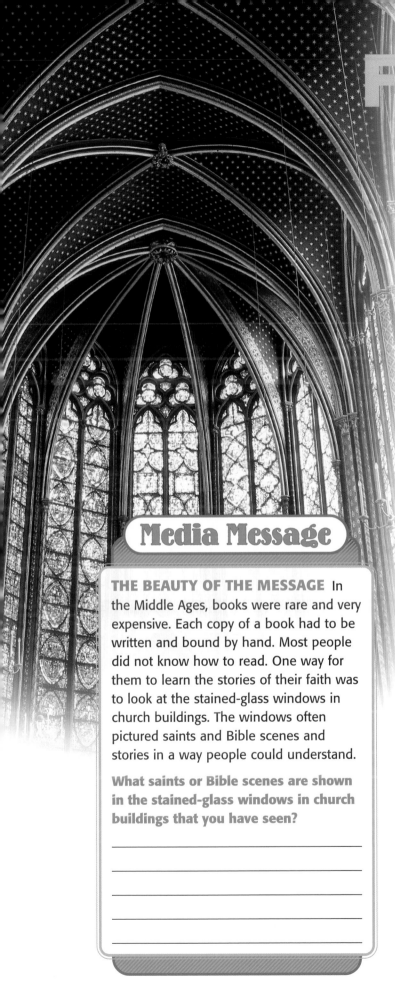

Faith and Art

During the early Middle Ages, daily life was hard and unstable. The peasants worked in the fields, and landowners were often at war. Art and education did not receive much attention. But through local monasteries, the Church continued to sponsor and develop art, share religious knowledge, and tend to the physical, mental, and spiritual needs of the community.

Monasticism is a way of life in which a group of men or women live in community so that they can give themselves to God more fully. Christian monasticism developed around A.D. 300 with Anthony of Egypt and was soon reinterpreted for the Church in the East by Basil. However, monasticism was further developed by Benedict in the sixth century and is most often associated with the Middle Ages.

Monasteries were central to many medieval towns and villages. Monks spent hours each day in prayer and reflection, copied and illustrated books, developed new medicines, improved farming techniques, and educated local townspeople. Monasteries provided food and shelter for travelers and so served as important sources of news.

Most of the art created during the Middle Ages was religious. Gregorian chant, a form of music used to accompany the text of the Mass, developed during the Middle Ages. The visual arts of painting, sculpture, and stained glass were often used to express faith. Many works were made possible by *patrons of the arts,* individuals and groups, including the Church, who provided money to support artists. The Middle Ages also witnessed an abundance of religious architecture, especially in the Romanesque and Gothic cathedrals.

Media Message

THE BEAUTY OF THE MESSAGE In the Middle Ages, books were rare and very expensive. Each copy of a book had to be written and bound by hand. Most people did not know how to read. One way for them to learn the stories of their faith was to look at the stained-glass windows in church buildings. The windows often pictured saints and Bible scenes and stories in a way people could understand.

What saints or Bible scenes are shown in the stained-glass windows in church buildings that you have seen?

_____
_____
_____
_____
_____

Discuss with your Faith Partner what you would like or dislike about monastic life.

Christians and Muslims Tensions between the followers of Christianity and the followers of Islam have been around for centuries. Islamic armies conquered Syria, Palestine, Egypt, and North Africa during the seventh century and conquered parts of Spain early in the eighth century. Then in A.D. 732 the governor of Cordoba, Spain, led his Islamic troops into war, with the goal of expanding into France. The French army resisted the invasion, and the two armies fought in a series of engagements that are known as the Battle of Tours, or the Battle of Poitiers. Eventually, the French broke through the Arab line, and the Spanish governor was killed. Islamic armies were not strong enough to attempt another invasion of France. Some historians today see great importance in the Battle of Tours because the victory of the Christian army kept Europe from becoming part of the Islamic empire.

For further information: Consult an encyclopedia, the Internet, or a history of Spain to learn about attempts by Muslim armies to invade Europe.

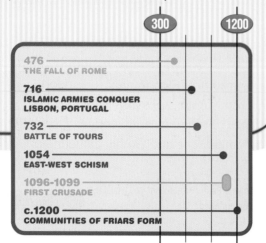

300   1200

476
THE FALL OF ROME

716
ISLAMIC ARMIES CONQUER
LISBON, PORTUGAL

732
BATTLE OF TOURS

1054
EAST-WEST SCHISM

1096-1099
FIRST CRUSADE

c.1200
COMMUNITIES OF FRIARS FORM

Conflicts and
Schism

Even though the old Roman Empire had fallen apart, the Church was still unified until around 1054. About that time there was a split between the Church in the East and the Church in the West. This split is called the **East-West Schism,** and it came about because of differences in doctrine, culture, politics, authority, and language. Today the Churches in the East form what is known as Orthodox Christianity. There are Churches in the East that are in union with Rome today. These are referred to as Eastern Catholic Churches.

In 1095 the emperor in the East asked to be saved from an invading Muslim army. The pope in the West called for a *crusade,* a military war, to reclaim Jerusalem so that Christians could visit holy places there. Unfortunately some of the soldiers who participated were looking for adventure and profit and disregarded the Church's goals. The First Crusade (1096–1099) rescued the Holy Land from the Turks, but only after misguided soldiers killed many innocent people along the way and threatened Constantinople. Later Crusades were just as bloody but often did not result in military success. By 1187 the Muslims were back in the Holy Land and had regained Jerusalem. During the fourth Crusade (1202–1204), soldiers invaded and looted Constantinople. The Crusades spanned nearly three hundred years but failed to achieve many of the goals promoted by the Church. They are now seen as part of an unfortunate, violent time in history, but they did serve to open many routes for trade, travel, and exploration.

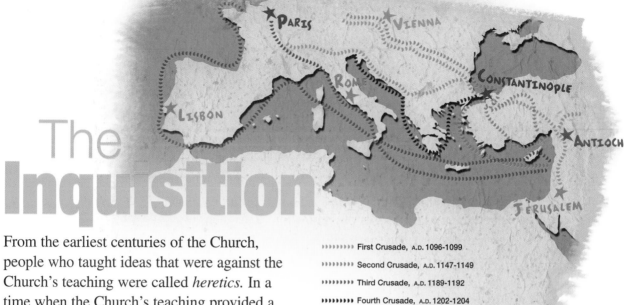

The Inquisition

From the earliest centuries of the Church, people who taught ideas that were against the Church's teaching were called *heretics.* In a time when the Church's teaching provided a basis for law and order, heresy was a crime against the state and the Church. In 1233 the pope appointed a special Church court to carry out an *inquisition* to question suspected heretics and encourage them to return to the beliefs of the Church. Sadly some of the men on these courts misused their power to punish suspected heratics with confiscation of property, imprisonment, torture, and even death.

Today we recognize that some of the people conducting inquisitions acted unjustly. In March 2000 Pope John Paul II made a public apology to the world for all the cruelties committed by Christians in the Crusades and the Inquisition.

A Church Crisis

By the fourteenth century conflicts between France and Italy led to a disagreement about the election of popes. The king of France moved the papacy to Avignon, France. In response, Italian bishops claimed that they had elected their own pope. For more than thirty years, there was a pope and another who claimed to be pope; eventually still another sought to be recognized as pope. This was the **Great Western Schism** (1378–1417). Finally, the bishops met in the Council of Constance. The pope and the two who claimed to be pope were rejected, and a new pope was elected.

▶▶▶▶▶▶ First Crusade, A.D. 1096-1099
▶▶▶▶▶▶ Second Crusade, A.D. 1147-1149
▶▶▶▶▶▶ Third Crusade, A.D. 1189-1192
▶▶▶▶▶▶ Fourth Crusade, A.D. 1202-1204

The Crusades and the schism changed Europe and opened up new possibilities for government, trade, and exploration. Towns began to grow, and conditions improved as craftsmen organized *guilds,* or associations. The guilds helped workers in times of sickness and death and set standards for good workmanship. New religious communities of *friars* were founded for active ministry to those in the developing cities.

The Church guided Europe through a demanding time in the Middle Ages. Many people gained a new appreciation of art, architecture, and learning as ways to honor God.

Catholics Believe

The Holy Spirit works in the Church through the sacraments and through the gifts and talents we have to share. See Catechism, #798.

What gifts do you think the Church especially needs today?

_____

_____

_____

Looking Back

Our world is still influenced by the Middle Ages. At some time in our lives, we may be able to travel to Europe and pray and worship in some of the cathedrals and monasteries from that earlier period. We can appreciate the art and music that express the Christian faith as it was lived then. Many works of architecture and art in our own country are patterned after those of Christian Europe. We can visit the universities begun centuries ago. The Church and the saints of the Middle Ages influenced their world and made it a better place.

The Church still helps shape who we are and is still a powerful voice in our world. Today a pope is much more likely to be a pilgrim for peace than the organizer of a crusade. He will speak out on issues of importance to the Church and society. Today we see the influence of the Church in our lives and in our culture every time there is an effort to bring justice to society, to care for people who are poor or sick, to protect the rights of people who are powerless or persecuted. The Holy Spirit acts among Christians today to help us understand our faith and work for unity among Christians and for cooperation with people of other religions and cultures.

Reflect on the influence of the Church in our lives and in our culture. Share your thoughts with your Faith Partner.

FaiTH PaRTNeRSHiP

WRAP UP

- Monasticism is a way of life in which a group of men or women live as a community so they can give themselves to God more fully.
- The Middle Ages were a period of great creativity for the Church.
- During the Middle Ages, Christendom became the main civilizing force.
- The Church in the East and the Church in the West split in 1054. This was called the East-West Schism.
- The Great Western Schism was a crisis of authority in the Church.

What questions do you have about the content of this chapter?

_____

_____

_____

Around the Group

Discuss the following question as a group.

What are the major contributions of the Middle Ages that are still with us today?

After everyone has had a chance to share his or her responses, come up with a group answer upon which everyone can agree.

_____

_____

_____

_____

What personal observations do you have about the group discussion and answer?

_____

_____

_____

_____

Briefly...

At the beginning of this chapter, you were asked to consider your own gifts and abilities. In light of your own talents and those of your peers, what contributions can your generation make to aid the Church and the culture?

_____

_____

_____

Social Analysis

Expressions of Faith—

The Christians of the Middle Ages built a Christian society as they shared their gifts and talents. They may have had ideas and responses that we do not agree with today, but they lived their faith in the best way they knew. They looked at the world around them and analyzed it to see how they could best respond to the needs of their time. The skill of Social Analysis helps us become aware of the world around us and how others live. In this way, it helps us live our faith by preparing us to actively participate in meeting the needs of our time.

Scripture

May the God of steadfastness and encouragement grant you to live in harmony with one another, in accordance with Christ Jesus.

Romans 15:5   2nd Sunday of Advent, Cycle A

Think About It—

The Christian living skill of Social Analysis challenges us to look beyond the narrow borders of our personal "world." We need to look beyond our families, friends, school, and town. We even need to look beyond our nation. As Christians we are called to be responsible for the welfare of the entire world. Look at the following and suggest one possible result of the action listed.

○ Richer parishes are asked to support poorer parishes.

Result: _____

○ Freedom of every kind of speech is allowed on the Internet.

Result: _____

○ All guns are made illegal.

Result: _____

○ The United Nations passes a resolution to ban all child labor.

Result: _____

○ The United States stops protecting other countries.

Result: _____

○ Your state passes a law that anyone polluting the environment faces stiff penalties and possible imprisonment.

Result: _____

Skill Steps-

The skill of Social Analysis can be difficult to practice. We might think we have the right answers and then find out we have overlooked something. We might not understand the whole situation in another part of the world. Sometimes we try to act before we completely think through our ideas. Use the following method when trying to use the skill of Social Analysis.

Look	Listen
Look up: Notice what is going on in the world.	*Listen before* you make up your mind.
Look into the issues people are talking about: read, watch, or listen to the news.	*Listen to* what people you trust are saying.
Look behind the information to see why people are involved in an issue.	*Listen for* what the Church and the Bible have to say.
Look beyond what is printed or broadcast on TV or radio for other information or opinions.	*Listen to* what is being said by people you don't know.

Ask	Act
Ask questions: Why does the situation exist? What contributes to it? Who can influence it?	*Act by* expressing your opinion.
Ask yourself to think about an issue.	*Act on* a situation when you can.
Ask God in prayer.	*Act locally* by doing something.
Ask about the consequences: Who is hurt? Who is helped? What would Jesus do?	*Act in* writing so people become aware.
	Act with a group to get more done.
	Act for those involved by praying.

Check It Out-

Place a check mark next to the sentences that apply to you.

◯ I learn what the Church and the Bible have to say.

◯ I listen to what others say before making up my mind.

◯ I pray for those involved in world events and for world leaders.

◯ I know what I believe in and what I stand for.

◯ I ask God for wisdom in understanding current issues.

Based on your responses, what kinds of things do you need to work on?

_____

_____

Closing Prayer-

*Lord, be with us as we become **aware** of the needs of the world. Guide us to **seek** ways to live in **peace** with one another. Help us use wisely all that you have graciously given us. Amen.*

The Church Is Challenged

Jesus, it isn't always easy to follow you. Sometimes we are criticized by others, and sometimes we are not sure what to do. Give us courage, and continue to guide us. May we live with hope and patience. Amen.

What three kinds of challenges do you think people face most often?

_____

_____

_____

How do you usually react when faced with a challenge related to something that is important to you?

- ○ See it as an opportunity
- ○ Hope it will go away
- ○ Think about what you can do
- ○ Meet it head-on
- ○ Other: _____

- ○ Complain about it
- ○ Worry about it
- ○ Talk it over with someone you respect
- ○ Pretend it isn't there

Open to
Challenge

Facing a challenge can be stressful and frightening, but it can also give us an opportunity to use our talents and wisdom. A challenge can help us clarify why something is important. It can motivate us to make a difference and even to make the world a better place. When we trust the Holy Spirit to guide us in facing a challenge, our faith deepens. Our beliefs and ideals help us make the right choices and support us when we are called to do something new or difficult.

Centuries ago the Church was challenged to respond in new ways to changes taking place in the culture of the time. Some people feared this challenge and thought that the results could only make things worse. But the challenges provided a unique opportunity for the Church to change in some positive, life-giving ways.

The Call for Reform

Have you ever realized that an action of yours was wrong, and then decided not to do it again? This can also happen in organizations, and it happened in the Church during the Reformation. Throughout Europe leaders began to challenge some of the practices of the Church, and many people called for reform.

Martin Luther was an Augustinian priest and university professor who wanted the chance to debate with others some Church practices and teachings that he thought should be reconsidered. One of the things that Luther most objected to was the sale of **indulgences.** An indulgence is a reduction of the temporal punishment that results from a sin being forgiven. The Church's system of indulgences is now based on prayer, sorrow for sin, and the Sacrament of Reconciliation. But in Luther's time some claimed that indulgences could be bought. People believed that buying indulgences could lessen the punishment for sin in the afterlife. Luther tried to stop these abuses, but he was not successful.

In response to the selling of indulgences and other corruption within the Church, Martin Luther is said to have posted ninety-five theses, or statements, on the door of the castle church in Wittenberg, Germany, in 1517.

Luther believed that the Bible is the only authority for Christian life. His primary point was that God saves us and we can share in that salvation through our faith, which is a free gift from God. Therefore we do not earn a place in heaven by doing good apart from faith. This argument became known as **justification by faith.**

The Church disagreed with Luther's reliance on faith alone. Over time Luther also departed from Church teaching concerning original sin, Baptism removing original sin, and the true presence of Christ in the sacraments, especially the Eucharist. Church leaders tried to convince Luther to change his

Opening the Word

Ascension of the Lord

I pray that the God of our Lord Jesus Christ, the Father of glory, may give you a spirit of wisdom and revelation as you come to know him....
Ephesians 1:17

Read *Ephesians 1:15–23*, as well as *Matthew 14:22–33, 1 Corinthians 1:26–29,* and *Philemon 4–6.* What do these passages tell us about what it means to have faith?

_____

_____

_____

beliefs. But Luther would not agree, and in 1521 he was excommunicated and condemned as an outlaw. In spite of the Church's condemnation of Luther, some people began to worship and live their faith according to what he taught. They became known as Lutherans. The movement started by Martin Luther's teachings was the **Reformation,** and it resulted in new Christian Churches being formed. Those involved were called **Protestants,** a term that referred both to their protest and their witness.

In England King Henry VIII declared himself the supreme head on earth of the Church of England. He had lost a dispute with Pope Clement VII about annulling his marriage so that he could remarry. His first marriage had not produced a male heir to the throne, which he believed was required to hold his nation together. The Church of England's followers are called Anglicans, or Episcopalians. Over time many Protestant beliefs and practices were incorporated in the Church of England.

In 1536 John Calvin, another Protestant reformer, wrote the *Institutes of the Christian Religion,* which is still read and studied more than four hundred years later. Calvin emphasized the need to live moral lives and to simplify the way people worshiped. Contrary to Church teaching, however, he taught that God predetermined who is saved and who is not and that the way we live does not influence God's decision. Calvin's followers were called Calvinists and were members of the Reformed movement.

Eventually the Church in Rome held the **Council of Trent** (1545–1563) to defend and clarify major Church teachings and to discuss issues raised by the Protestants. During its twenty-five sessions, the council corrected some of the abuses that led to the Reformation and developed a comprehensive catechism. The council's work provided a foundation for Catholic teaching and practice for the next four hundred years, but it did not reunite the Church.

Castle church in Wittenberg, Germany

Our Christian Journey

A Most Important Meeting

Luther and others had called for a general Church council as early as 1520. The meeting was delayed for years by political disagreements among European nations and between the pope and the heads of certain nations. When the Council of Trent was finally held, Protestants decided not to attend. Most of the Church leaders who attended were Italian and Spanish bishops. The decrees of the Council of Trent resolved some of the problems addressed by the Protestant reformers and established seminaries for the formation and education of future priests.

For further information: Research the Second Vatican Council by using a Catholic encyclopedia or the Internet, and compare the number in attendance to the number attending the Council of Trent.

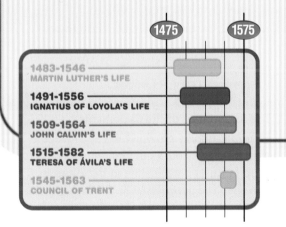

1475   1575

1483-1546
MARTIN LUTHER'S LIFE

1491-1556
IGNATIUS OF LOYOLA'S LIFE

1509-1564
JOHN CALVIN'S LIFE

1515-1582
TERESA OF ÁVILA'S LIFE

1545-1563
COUNCIL OF TRENT

The Catholic Reformation

Ignatius of Loyola

Some reformers left the Church or were excommunicated. Several of them established their own Protestant Churches. However, other reformers stayed in the Church and worked for reform. Many of them worked to improve the education of priests and establish schools and colleges. These dedicated Catholic reformers offered hope and inspiration to Catholics throughout Europe. People were encouraged to nourish their personal relationship with Jesus and to live their faith every day. Many books were written to give practical advice on how to pray, how to live a moral life, and how to serve others.

Ignatius of Loyola was a reformer who, through his writings, encouraged spiritual growth and renewal. His *Spiritual Exercises* offer practical spiritual advice and encourage readers to strengthen their faith. Ignatius also founded the religious order of the Jesuits. Men who were Jesuits established schools and colleges and worked as missionaries throughout the world, as they continue to do today.

Some reformers worked to encourage the spiritual life within religious orders. Teresa of Ávila worked with John of the Cross to reform the Carmelite Order, helping men and women religious lead lives of prayerful holiness. Teresa of Ávila was known for her intelligence and her sense of humor and is still a highly respected saint today. Both John and Teresa were **mystics** who wrote about prayer, meditation, and contemplation. Mystics are individuals who experience direct communication with God. This can happen during *contemplation,* a way of seeking God that is a prayer without words. During times of contemplation mystics may be given special knowledge about truth or the world.

Philip Neri, another person who worked for positive change within the Church, founded the Congregation of the Oratory to encourage good preaching and priestly lives of holiness. Philip Neri was a man of prayer whose generous spirit attracted many people and led them back to God. Ignatius of Loyola, Teresa of Ávila, John of the Cross, and Philip Neri are all canonized saints of the Catholic Church.

Rite Response

The Importance of the Sacraments

To help Catholics grow in faith and love, the bishops at the Council of Trent emphasized the importance of participation in the Eucharist. They reminded the people that in the Eucharist Catholics receive the strength to live the faith and that through the Eucharist lesser sins are forgiven. The council declared that the Eucharist should be celebrated frequently and serious sins confessed at least once a year.

Changes and **Choices**

When we are challenged, we sometimes feel that we need to fight back or run away. But there is a third possibility: sometimes we can stay and work with the people or the situation that is challenging us. Although the Catholic Reformation came too late to prevent grave divisions in the Christian Church, it helped the Catholic Church make many important and needed changes. The Church worked to eliminate corruption and began to explain its teachings more clearly. New religious orders arose to educate, to help people who were poor, and to care for those who were sick. Following the Holy Spirit's guidance, the Church took positive action and thus encouraged Catholics to grow stronger in their faith.

Catholics Believe

The purpose that governs everything in the Church is the unity of humans with God.

See Catechism, #773.

How does the Church work for the unity of God and humans?

_____

_____

_____

Share your responses and thoughts with your Faith Partner.

The Reformation changed Christendom for centuries to come. Within a short time there were now many Christian denominations, separated by disagreements on belief and church life. Today there are several hundred Christian denominations.

Eventually people recognized that a government cannot force someone to have faith or belong to a particular denomination. People began to value freedom of conscience and freedom of religion. The idea of the separation of church and state comes from this time period.

Calls for reform led the Church to identify abuses and to restore the Church to its mission of sharing the gospel message and leading the Christian faithful. The Reformation was a rocky period in our Christian story, but many people who responded to its challenges made changes that built up the Church as the Body of Christ.

- Catholicism
- Orthodox Christianity
- Anglicanism
- Calvinism
- Lutheranism

SWEDEN FINLAND

NORWAY RUSSIA

SCOTLAND DENMARK

IRELAND NETHERLANDS POLAND

ENGLAND GERMANY

AUSTRIA HUNGARY

FRANCE

OTTOMAN EMPIRE

PORTUGAL ITALY

SPAIN

A Challenge Is an Opportunity

What kinds of challenges are you facing? Is there some situation in which you need to be more open-minded and willing to respond to challenges? How can these qualities make your life better?

From the time of Jesus through the years of growth and persecution of the early Church, faithful Christians were continually challenged to apply the qualities of open-mindedness and willingness to change. In every generation the Holy Spirit challenges Christians to live their faith and to address the problems that the Church and the world face. In every age Christians are called to make the world a better place, to spread the good news of the gospel, and to work for the unity of all Christians in the one and only Church of Christ.

We can learn from the past how important it is to acknowledge one's mistakes and apply our Christian ideals to changing circumstances. To take on a challenge is to accept an opportunity. When we remember this, we can stay open to what will help build up the Church.

When we continue to nourish our relationship with God, we can look forward to facing whatever challenges we meet. We can trust the Holy Spirit to guide us and keep our faith strong. We can embrace the world, eager to share ourselves and our faith with everyone we meet.

Reflect on the importance of being open-minded and willing to make necessary changes. Share your thoughts with your Faith Partner.

WRAP UP

- The Council of Trent defended and clarified major Church teachings and reformed some Church practices.

- Martin Luther, John Calvin, and others led the Protestant Reformation.

- The Catholic Reformation helped the Church correct some abuses and encouraged a better realization of its original mission.

- Saints Ignatius of Loyola, Teresa of Ávila, Philip Neri, and others worked to renew the Catholic Church.

What questions do you have about the content of this chapter?

_____

_____

_____

Around the Group

Discuss the following questions as a group.

What do you see as the biggest challenges facing the Church today? What can you or your group do to bring about positive changes?

After everyone has had a chance to share his or her responses, focus on the second question and come up with a group answer upon which everyone can agree.

_____

_____

_____

_____

What personal observations do you have about the group discussion and answer?

_____

_____

_____

_____

Briefly...

At the beginning of this chapter, you were asked to consider how people respond to challenges. When you face a challenge, what motivates you to respond to it in a positive way?

_____

_____

_____

Social Analysis

Expressions of Faith–

As members of the Church, we have to practice the skill of Social Analysis to see whether we are doing all that we are called to do.

Skill Steps–

The skill of Social Analysis can help us respond to the needs of others and make our world a better place.

Here are some key points to remember from the previous chapter:

- **Look:** Look up from what you are doing; look into and behind the issues; and look beyond what you're being told.

- **Listen:** Listen before you make up your mind; listen to what you are being told; and listen for what the Church and the Bible say.

- **Ask:** Ask questions about an issue; ask God by spending time in prayer; and ask about the consequences.

- **Act:** Act by expressing your opinion; act when you have an opportunity to do something positive; act locally; act in writing; act with a group; and act for others by praying.

Skill Builder–

Imagine that you meet twice a year with all the bishops to discuss important issues, policies, and problems. You also meet privately with the pope every few years.

Share your responses and thoughts with your Faith Partner.

○ Name the two issues that the Church and the world face today that you would like to discuss with the other bishops or the pope.

_____

○ What information do you want to have before you decide?

_____

○ What actions would you suggest to the bishops or the pope?

_____

Putting It into Practice-

Practice the skill of Social Analysis by looking at the issue of capital punishment.

○ Look: Read several news articles about capital punishment. What opinions are being expressed in the articles?

_____

_____

○ Listen: Listen to what's being said about capital punishment, both by people you know and those you don't. What do the Church and the Bible say about it?

_____

_____

○ Ask: Get more information. Ask God for guidance. Ask who is hurt and who is helped by capital punishment.

_____

_____

○ Act: Express your opinion. Write a letter to the editor of your local newspaper. Pray with others for those who are on death row.

_____

_____

Social analysis is expected of us as God's people. To live our faith fully, we need to be aware of the world around us and how others live. The skill of Social Analysis helps us see whether we are doing all that we need to do to follow Jesus' teachings and respond to the Holy Spirit.

Now that you've had some practice using the skill of Social Analysis, list one aspect of the skill that you consider yourself good at and one that you still need to work on.

_____

_____

_____

Closing Prayer-

Come, **Holy Spirit**. Guide the leaders of all Christian Churches, and guide us as we grow in faith. Give us the wisdom, strength, and courage to make positive **changes** in our lives. Amen.

The Catholic Church Expands

Almighty God, your people face many challenges in today's world. Yet our faith in you remains strong, even when we are criticized or persecuted. Strengthen us, Lord.

Identify two emotions you have when you are inspired by something.

_____

_____

Sketch a symbol that represents something that inspires you.

Looking for
Strength

At many times in our personal stories, we are confronted by concerns or struggles that seem to put stumbling blocks on our path. To gain the wisdom and strength to deal with such problems, we can look to what inspires us. This may mean listening to favorite music, spending time with a friend, or simply enjoying a favorite poster or work of art. The things that motivate us help us feel energized to face challenges.

From the beginning of the Renaissance (fourteenth century) through the Enlightenment (eighteenth century), the Church was called to respond to drastic changes that were going on in the world. Catholics of that time found strength and wisdom in many sources of inspiration, such as the Mass, the Bible, and the art, architecture, and stained-glass windows of the great cathedrals.

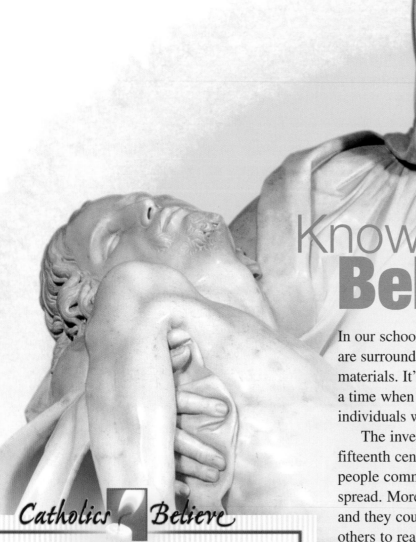

Knowing and
Believing

In our schools, churches, and homes, we are surrounded by books and other printed materials. It's hard for most of us to picture a time when only people in monasteries and individuals with great wealth were able to read.

The invention of the printing press in the fifteenth century completely changed the way people communicated and the way knowledge spread. More people could now read the Bible, and they could write their opinions down for others to read. One reason that Martin Luther's ideas spread quickly was that they were printed and then read by many people.

The Reformation happened during the **Renaissance.** This was the period from the fourteenth through the seventeenth centuries when many Europeans began to use the ancient Greeks and Romans as their models for art and architecture. Science, math, and other areas of learning advanced during the Renaissance. Scholars studied history and classical writers such as Cicero and Homer. They also studied Greek and Hebrew, the original languages of the Bible. Art and architecture flourished, giving the world such brilliant artists as Botticelli, da Vinci, and Michelangelo. In politics, many national governments began to form and grow strong.

Catholics Believe

God has begun his kingdom in Christ, and it continues in the Church. It will be complete at the end of time. See Catechism, #865.

Sketch a banner design that shows how the kingdom of God is present in today's Christian Church.

Scientific discoveries were made that affected and were affected by our Christian story. Nicolaus Copernicus found out that the sun was the center of the solar system. His discovery raised important questions. If the earth was not the center of the universe, then how important were humans? What was our role in the universe? Many people were seeing new possibilities for what humans could do. After all, they asked themselves, why did God give us these abilities if not to use them to explore the world and improve our lives?

This outlook is called **humanism,** a way of life that focuses on human interests, values, and capabilities. Humanists of the Renaissance believed that knowledge was good and should be used to make the world a better place.

Missions and
Expansion

Along with the growing hunger for knowledge came a desire to explore other lands and import raw materials from them. Before the Reformation, European powers such as Spain and Portugal had already begun to send merchants around the globe to trade. Countries competed for the best markets. The pope, the most powerful ruler in Europe at the time, thought it was fitting to divide up the world for Europeans to conquer. In 1454 Pope Nicholas V granted the Portuguese the right to control the west coast of Africa. Then in 1493, after the Spanish discovery of the Americas, Pope Alexander VI took a map and drew a line from pole to pole, giving everything west of the line to Spain and everything east of the line to Portugal. This is why Mexico, Central America, and much of South America were originally settled by the Spanish, while the Portuguese settled in what is now Brazil.

OUR CHRISTIAN JOURNEY

A Communications Milestone Before the printing press, making books was a slow, difficult, and expensive process. Pages were created by hand, one at a time, and then all the pages were sewn together. Printing with hand-carved wooden blocks had been known for centuries, but it had not been possible to carve out an entire page of text using that method. Johannes Gutenberg experimented with various sizes of individual metal letters, which were durable enough to be used for printing many copies. In about 1455 he succeeded in attaching the metal letters to a machine similar to a wine press to make the first printing press. Gutenberg produced individual letters that resembled the calligraphy letters used by monks and other scribes for their hand-lettered, highly decorated manuscripts of the Bible. The first book ever printed on Gutenberg's press was the Bible. We don't know how many Bibles were printed by Gutenberg, but forty copies of that early printing still survive.

For further information: Use a book on inventions or the Internet to research the scientific achievements and inventions of the Renaissance.

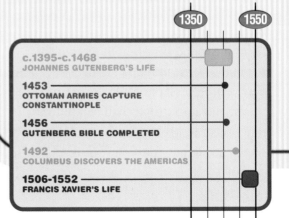

1350   1550

c.1395-c.1468
JOHANNES GUTENBERG'S LIFE

1453
OTTOMAN ARMIES CAPTURE CONSTANTINOPLE

1456
GUTENBERG BIBLE COMPLETED

1492
COLUMBUS DISCOVERS THE AMERICAS

1506-1552
FRANCIS XAVIER'S LIFE

When kings conquered a people, they sent missionaries to Christianize them. Native religions were considered "pagan" and sometimes even Satanic. At that point in history, being conquered often meant being forced to convert to Christianity.

Missionaries followed traders to Africa, India, Japan, China, and North and South America. Francis Xavier was one of the missionaries to the Far East who did not use force. Wherever he went, he learned the local language so that he could translate Christian beliefs and teach the people what it meant to be Christian. Francis saw children as the hope of all his missionary work. In each culture he visited, he put Christian beliefs into rhymed verse and songs, so that young children could sing the faith even before they understood it. By teaching the children, he planted seeds of faith that could grow as the children did. Francis Xavier worked as a missionary in India for seven years and in Japan for two years. But he died before he reached his goal of working in China.

Everywhere the missionaries went, they tried to create strong Christian communities. Sometimes they required new Christians to live in villages where they could pray and work and live a common life. The missionaries often lived in places that required great sacrifice, hard work, and heroism. They frequently faced danger and sometimes were martyred for their faith. They helped the Church expand throughout the world.

The seventeenth and eighteenth centuries were a time of exploration and a time of royal power. Because armies had begun to use gunpowder to protect lands, castles were no longer needed as fortresses. Instead, they

Our Global Community

Power and Authority

The growth of knowledge, especially in science and mathematics, helped Europe become stronger and wealthier. It also helped European nations spread their influence throughout the world. By 1800 Europeans had created an international system of money and trade. They had established settlements throughout the world. Europeans used their knowledge and their political and military force to control other peoples. For example, they were heavily involved in the African slave trade. Through its system of colonies, Europe dominated the world from this period until after World War II.

became palaces and were decorated as elegantly as possible in a style called Baroque, which was meant to dazzle and overwhelm. Many Baroque paintings and buildings had religious themes that showed the glory of the Church as well as the power of kings. The classical influence of Rome and Greece can also be seen in churches and public buildings built during this time. Once the Church was divided in the Reformation, the king of each country decided what religion his people would follow. Between 1600 and 1800 kings held power over the Church in their countries. Consequently, for most people of that time, the pope became a distant figure with little influence.

The Enlightenment

In addition to the changes in the Church and in governments, advances in knowledge, especially in scientific areas, were continuing to amaze people everywhere. People believed in the power of knowledge to change the world, and they became more optimistic about life. They began to experience how knowledge could change the way they thought about themselves and the way they viewed the world. For instance, if the human body could be studied, then possibly diseases could be cured. If disease could be cured by medicine, then perhaps disease was not caused by sin. If disease and suffering were not punishment for sin, then how did God act in a human's life? What does it mean to be good or bad? To lead a moral life? How are humans to treat one another?

During the eighteenth century people began to rely heavily on reason and on their ever-growing knowledge of the physical world. That is why this period is known as the **Enlightenment,** or the Age of Reason. During this time some people sought to discover how the Bible had been written and by whom. They wanted to learn more about what specific passages in the Bible meant and how Jesus had lived on earth. People began to respect differences of opinion and to show *tolerance* by peacefully relating to others who disagreed. Slowly, ideas about human rights began to take shape, and freedom of conscience became important.

What developments of the Enlightenment period do you see as influencing people today? Share your thoughts with your Faith Partner.

Faith and Progress

However, not all of the new ideas that arose after the Renaissance were respectful of Church beliefs. Church leaders found it difficult to accept many of the changes happening in the world. Catholic popes and bishops believed that tolerance would go too far if it led people to accept harmful ideas. Mistrust developed, and it became harder and harder for people to see how faith and progress could go together.

The progress that had been made since the Renaissance had resulted in better living conditions for many. Some Catholics realized that many of the new ideas and inventions could be used responsibly to improve life for everyone.

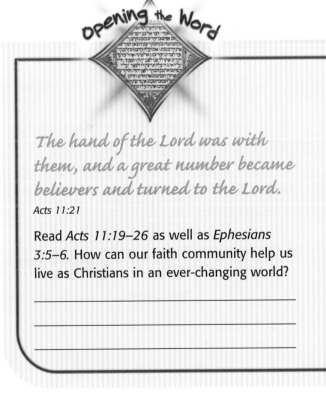

Opening the Word

The hand of the Lord was with them, and a great number became believers and turned to the Lord.
Acts 11:21

Read *Acts 11:19–26* as well as *Ephesians 3:5–6.* How can our faith community help us live as Christians in an ever-changing world?

_____

_____

_____

Keeping the **Faith**

The Renaissance and the Enlightenment led people to appreciate how God-given talents and abilities can be used for the good of people and the world. People shared knowledge and discussed ideas. Some forms of acquiring knowledge, such as the study of the Bible, helped Christians understand their faith better.

Some serious challenges to faith also developed during this period. There were individuals who rejected religion and the Church completely. Some people said that religion could not be true because religious beliefs could not be proven as scientific ideas could be. Others asked questions such as: What is the meaning of suffering? What does it mean to lead a moral life? How are we to treat one another?

We face similar challenges in living our Christian story. As Catholics, we need to continue asking God to guide us through our learning at each stage of our personal story. God provides us with teachers, mentors, friends, and situations that help us examine our beliefs more deeply. Many people who are seventy or eighty years old admit, "My faith is still growing." God is part of every aspect of our lives—life teaches us about God, and God teaches us about life.

Think about the questions you have about your life and faith. What adults do you know who might help you explore your questions?

Reflect on current challenges to your beliefs and how you might respond. Share your thoughts with your Faith Partner.

FaiTH PaRTNeRSHiP

WRAP UP

- •Because of the Renaissance, many people appreciated progress more and concentrated on how they could use their gifts and talents.

- •Missionaries followed traders throughout the world to spread the gospel.

- •Some strong kings limited the Church's influence in their kingdoms; others expanded it.

- •During the Enlightenment people raised questions about the purpose of life and the meaning of faith.

What questions do you have about the content of this chapter?

_____

_____

_____

Discuss the following questions as a group.

In what ways can young people today find strength and inspiration for their faith? How can young people be sources of strength and inspiration for others?

After everyone has had a chance to share his or her responses, focus on the second question and come up with a group answer upon which everyone can agree.

_____

_____

_____

_____

What personal observations do you have about the group discussion and answer?

_____

_____

_____

_____

Briefly...

At the beginning of this chapter, you were asked to consider what inspires you. Now take some time to consider two events or problems that confuse you or challenge your faith. List them below, and plan a time to share your concerns with a family member or mentor.

_____

_____

SKILLS FOR Christian Living

Making Changes

Expressions of Faith—

Many changes took place in the world between the Renaissance and the Enlightenment, and the Church had to decide how to respond. The Church reacted against many of the changes. However, eventually Church leaders realized that some major changes were necessary. Then their challenge was to make these changes in a way that would help people grow in their understanding and practice of the Catholic faith.

Scripture

We know that all things work together for good for those who love God, who are called according to his purpose.
Romans 8:28

17th Sunday of
Ordinary Time, Cycle A

Think About It—

Making changes is a big part of our lives. Seasons change. Our interests change. Friends decide to do things differently. People grow older. If we are to grow, we must change. Use this exercise to look at your own experience of change.

○ Describe a major change that has happened to you in the past five years—a change within yourself or your family, in your school life, or with friends.

_____
_____
_____

○ What changes have happened to you that you have enjoyed?

_____
_____
_____

○ What changes have been difficult for you to cope with?

_____
_____
_____

Skill Steps-

You already know a lot about the skill of Making Changes. But sometimes changes seem frightening or difficult. You can deal with your discomfort by taking an active role in making decisions rather than letting life happen to you.
These reminders can help you make changes.

● Change is natural.

● Changes bring up strong emotions.

● You can take an active role in making changes.

● Change often leads to growth.

● When you choose to make changes, you have more to say about how and when the changes take place.

Think about the advice you would give someone else about making changes—then give that same advice to yourself! **Name several things you think someone your age should keep in mind when making changes.** For example, we can remember to be true to our faith.

_____

_____

_____

Check It Out-

Place a check mark next to the sentences that apply to you.

○ Change makes things interesting.

○ Change is easy for me.

○ I hate change.

○ If I need to make a change, I think about what's involved.

○ I let changes happen rather than make changes happen.

○ I've experienced a lot of tough changes.

Based on your responses, what can you do that will help you make changes?

_____

_____

Closing Prayer-

Lord, thank you for giving the Church the wisdom and courage to speak to the world. Help us make the world a just place for all of God's people. Amen.

The Church in the Americas

Father, look with love upon us when we gather together to praise you and worship you. Help us be generous and keep our faith communities strong. Draw us ever closer to you. We ask this in Jesus' name. Amen.

Our Church

Think about your parish. What regular activities and special events do you and other family members participate in? How well do you know other members of the community?

You or your friends may volunteer as altar servers or lectors and participate in youth activities. You gather with the rest of the community to celebrate the Eucharist every week. Being part of a faith community is a very important part of being Catholic. We are members of the Body of Christ. We belong to the same community of believers as the early Christians who were persecuted centuries ago. We belong to the same community for which Thomas Aquinas wrote and Teresa of Ávila prayed. We are connected to all the people of the past because, like them, we are members of the Christian Church. We contribute our faith experience to the ongoing Christian story.

Expansion Continues

In their search for wealth, Spanish *conquistadors,* or conquerors, began arriving in the Americas in the sixteenth century. These leaders of raiding parties wanted to conquer the peoples so they could take their natural resources and send those resources back to Spain. The conquistadors set up governments, and settlers arrived to live permanently in these conquered lands, which eventually became colonies under Spanish control. Many Spanish settlers brought African slaves across the Atlantic to work the land. Times were hard in the Spanish colonies, and there was much injustice.

Missionaries who had arrived with the explorers continued to work in the new world of the Americas. Sixteenth-century ideas about the **universality** of the Church had led people to expect that everyone living in newly explored lands would become Christian. Franciscans, Dominicans, and Jesuits came to Spanish colonies in North America and South America to preach among the Native Americans. Missions were begun in Mexico and soon existed in many parts of South America.

Opening the Word

And he said to them, "Go into all the world and proclaim the good news to the whole creation."
Mark 16:15

Read *Mark 16:15, 20* as well as *Acts 2:22–24* and *2 Corinthians 5:17–21*. In the space below, create an advertisement that communicates the good news expressed in these passages.

Lay missionaries, those who are not ordained or part of a religious community, are given the authority to announce the gospel to those who have not heard it and to further educational, social, and medical developments in underdeveloped areas.

Like the Spanish conquistadors, the French sought to discover and claim much of the new world. French explorers and adventurers came to North America and traveled the waterways of the St. Lawrence River and the Great Lakes. Jesuit missionaries followed them, working mainly with Algonquins, Hurons, and Iroquois. The missionaries knew they might be persecuted as the early Christians had been. In fact, between 1642 and 1649, eight Jesuits were martyred.

Father Jacques Marquette preached in Michigan and Wisconsin and accompanied Louis Jolliet, the French explorer who discovered that the Mississippi River flowed into the Gulf of Mexico. Marguerite Bourgeoys came from France to Canada and founded the Congregation of Notre Dame, a religious order for women. Hundreds of other religious communities of men and women eventually flourished in the Americas. By the mid-nineteenth century Catholics in Canada enjoyed freedom of religion.

In the western part of what is now the United States, Junipero Serra and other missionaries taught Native Americans basic Spanish and new work skills. Some missionaries, such as Eusebio Kino, tried to include Native American language and culture in their efforts to spread the faith.

Although some missionaries were guilty of abusing native peoples, many missionaries worked to protect them from being enslaved, overworked, and treated cruelly by the settlers. Over the centuries missionaries have faced difficult decisions during times of violence, corruption, political revolution, and tension among people of different races. They have also been called on to deal with conflicts between people who are very rich and people who are very poor. Today, many missionaries in Latin America work against corruption to bring people justice, peace, and hope.

Focus On

Celebrating Joyfully

Catholics in Mexico celebrate Christmas with *La Posada* parties. Each night between December 16 and 24, people walk in procession from house to house, recalling how Mary and Joseph looked for shelter in Bethlehem. Candles are lit and songs are sung. Each night one family welcomes the participants in the procession into their home as part of the celebration.

OUR CHRISTIAN JOURNEY

A Young Woman of Faith Kateri Tekakwitha was born in what is now New York state. She is called the Lily of the Mohawks. Her father was a member of the Mohawk nation, and her mother was a Christian Algonquin. Kateri was very young when her parents died, and she barely survived a smallpox epidemic. Her face was disfigured by the disease, and her eyesight was impaired. Relatives took her in and raised her. On Easter Sunday in 1676, Kateri was baptized a Catholic. Her relatives were furious that she had become a Catholic, and she was forced to flee to the Mission of Saint Francis Xavier near Montreal, Canada. Kateri lived there for several years, teaching children and living a holy life. She died at the age of twenty-four and is remembered as a gentle and kind Native American woman of great faith. She was beatified in 1980, and her feast day is July 14.

For further information: Learn more about Kateri Tekakwitha by reading a biography or researching the Internet.

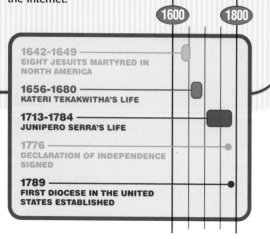

1600   **1800**

1642-1649
EIGHT JESUITS MARTYRED IN NORTH AMERICA

1656-1680
KATERI TEKAKWITHA'S LIFE

1713-1784
JUNIPERO SERRA'S LIFE

1776
DECLARATION OF INDEPENDENCE SIGNED

1789
FIRST DIOCESE IN THE UNITED STATES ESTABLISHED

The Church in the United States

The United States officially formed after the American Revolution against England in the late eighteenth century. Of the original thirteen English colonies, only Pennsylvania (settled by Quakers) and Maryland (settled by Catholics) allowed freedom of religion for Catholics. However, once the First Amendment of the Constitution was passed, freedom of religion was allowed throughout the country. Christian Churches grew and the gospel spread rapidly.

In 1789 the first Catholic **diocese** was formed in Maryland. The geographical area around Maryland's largest city became the Diocese of Baltimore, with John Carroll as its bishop. Bishop Carroll invited Elizabeth Ann Seton to open a school for girls in Baltimore, and she eventually began the Sisters of Charity to teach young women. Elizabeth Ann Seton was canonized in 1975 and was the first U.S.-born person to be declared a saint.

Smaller areas within dioceses were designated as **parishes,** and each parish was entrusted to the care of a priest, or pastor. Because of the small number of priests, some parishes were owned and run by lay people who were trustees, or caretakers, for the Church. As the Church grew, frequent disagreements arose between trustees, priests, and bishops about how things should be done. Some trustees wanted to make decisions for their parishes without consulting the priests and bishops who governed the Church.

Beginning about 1850 the Catholic Church in North America experienced a period of rapid growth because of the arrival of large numbers of immigrants—first from Ireland, Germany, and Italy, and later from Poland and other Eastern European countries. These groups of immigrants faced the difficult task of establishing parishes, schools, hospitals, and colleges. They often wrote back to their countries of origin to ask priests and religious sisters to come to the "new world" to help them.

The bishops of the United States worked hard to help the immigrants build good lives. They decided that every parish should have a school that would help Catholics continue to have a strong faith. In 1884 the bishops began an extensive system of Catholic schools. The bishops also published the *Baltimore Catechism,* which was written in question-and-answer format so that children could learn essential beliefs and practices of the Catholic Church.

Some non-Catholics thought that Catholics could not be loyal citizens if they obeyed the authority of the pope in Rome. There were cases of discrimination and violence against Catholics, and in some cases their property was destroyed. Some Catholics died as a result of these incidents. Immigrants also faced prejudice from Catholics who had lived in the United States for a generation or more and from Catholics of other ethnic groups.

In spite of the prejudices and discrimination they faced, Catholics banded together to help themselves and others. Many Catholics worked long hours in bad conditions in factories and coal mines. James Cardinal Gibbons, the archbishop of Baltimore, worked with the Knights of Labor—one of the first labor unions in the United States—to improve those conditions. Rose Philippine Duchesne established schools for girls and lived and prayed among Native Americans in Kansas. Katharine Drexel dedicated her life to improving conditions for African Americans and Native Americans. She began the Sisters of the Blessed Sacrament to help carry on this work and founded Xavier University of New Orleans, the only predominantly black Catholic university in the Western Hemisphere. John H. Dorsey, one of the first African American priests, spent much of his life working among African Americans in the South.

By the end of the twentieth century, many Hispanic Catholics were also part of the Church in the United States. Other Catholic immigrants came from the Caribbean islands, Central America, Africa, and Asia. Today the Catholic Church is the largest Christian denomination in the country, making up nearly one quarter of the American population.

Discuss with your Faith Partner the ethnic diversity of your parish or school.

FaiTH PaRTNeRSHiP

Catholics Believe

The Church has been given the mission to bring all people into communion with God—Father, Son, and Holy Spirit.
See Catechism, #850.

Name one way the Church carries out its mission in the world today.

_____

Being Catholic in the United States

Catholics in the United States enjoy many freedoms. In this country the Church can own property and build schools and churches. Catholics can freely publish religious books, magazines, and newspapers. They can produce television shows and create Web sites about Catholicism.

The Catholic Church in the United States is known for its strong educational system. More than 5 percent of the colleges and universities and 10 percent of the elementary schools in this country are Catholic. Catholic schools and colleges have a reputation for excellence and high achievement. Notre Dame and Georgetown are two well-known Catholic universities.

Catholics in the United States play an active role in society. Groups such as Catholics Against Capital Punishment inform both the public and lawmakers about the Church's teaching regarding the immorality of the death penalty. Similar groups of Catholics organize and gather to influence public policy on abortion and other important issues. Through such efforts Catholics in the United States influence others to do good.

Reflect on the advantages and disadvantages of being Catholic in the United States today. Share your thoughts with your Faith Partner.

FaiTH ParTNeRSHiP

WRAP UP

- **Missionaries from Europe began to preach the gospel to Native Americans in the sixteenth century.**
- **The Catholic Church in the United States grew through the rapid arrival of large numbers of immigrants.**
- **The Catholic Church in the United States has sometimes experienced anti-Catholic prejudice.**
- **Today the Catholic Church is the largest and most influential Christian denomination in the United States.**

What questions do you have about the content of this chapter?

_____

_____

_____

Around the Group

Discuss the following question as a group.

What celebrations in your city or community have Catholic roots?

After everyone has had a chance to share his or her responses, come up with a group answer upon which everyone can agree.

_____
_____
_____

What personal observations do you have about the group discussion and answer?

_____
_____
_____
_____

Briefly...

At the beginning of this chapter, you were asked for information about your faith community. If you were getting acquainted with a new friend's family members, how would they know you are Catholic?

_____
_____
_____

Protesters demonstrate against capital punishment.

Making Changes

Expressions of Faith—

Making changes is an important part of our Christian story. Sometimes making changes means taking action, and other times it means changing our attitudes. Jesus taught that by making spiritual changes we can grow in other aspects of our lives. Making spiritual changes can help us live a faithful, moral life and can give us a sense of peace and a spirit of gratitude for the little things in life.

Scripture

"Do not store up for yourselves treasures on earth, where moth and rust consume and where thieves break in and steal; but store up for yourselves treasures in heaven, where neither moth nor rust consumes and where thieves do not break in and steal. For where your treasure is, there your heart will be also."

Matthew 6:19–21

Skill Steps—

As long as you live, you will face changes. But you don't have to sit back and let life happen to you. **You can take an active role in making changes.** You can choose to make changes that are likely to lead in good directions.

These reminders can help you make changes.

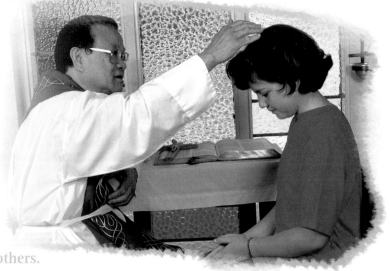

- Change is a natural part of being human.
- You can take an active role in your life by deciding what changes you want to make rather than letting life happen to you.
- Making changes can be stressful, but it can also lead you to new opportunities.
- When you keep in mind what is important to you, you are more likely to make changes that will improve your life and the lives of others.
- Some changes will strengthen your faith, while others may weaken your relationship with God.

Skill Builder-

Some changes are spiritual. Reread *Matthew 6:19–21*. Think of a change you would like to make in your life. Consider making a positive change regarding your relationship with God, how you practice your Catholic faith, or the way you follow Jesus' teachings in your everyday life.

○ Review the Chapter 7 *Skill Steps*. Write what you will need to do or keep in mind to make this spiritual change.

_____

_____

The skill of Making Changes can help you plan changes that you want to make. It can also help you adapt when someone else makes changes that affect you. You may find this skill useful when you want to change something about how you relate to friends or family members, do your schoolwork, or spend your free time.

Putting It into Practice-

Identify an important change you need or want to make within the next two months. This change may involve your friendships, your family members, or schoolwork. It may include changes in your attitudes or your behavior.

_____

_____

Using what you have learned about making changes, outline what you will do or keep in mind. Consult the list of reminders from *Skill Steps* in Chapter 7 and the *Skill Builder* exercise above.

_____

_____

_____

_____

List which aspects of this skill you do well and which you want to improve.

_____

_____

Closing Prayer-

God of hope, show us how we can meet the challenge of doing things that are new or difficult. Help us appreciate our heritage and our lives as Catholics in the United States. Amen.

The Church in the Modern World

Gracious Creator, you are all-knowing and all-powerful. Glory to you. Jesus, thank you for becoming one of us. Holy Spirit, help us lead holy lives. Remember your Church, and shower your love upon all of us.

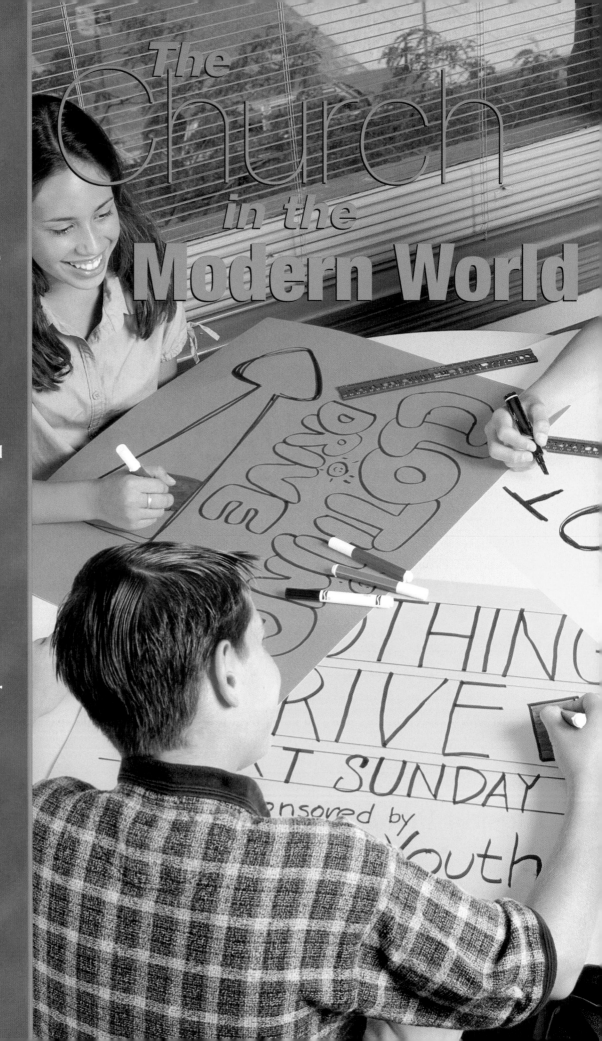

List the three or four electronic devices you use most often.

_____

_____

_____

_____

Which one of these is most important to you, and why?

_____

_____

_____

_____

_____

The Gifts
Of Technology

Developments of the past thirty years have made the cell phone, pager, compact disc (CD), digital videodisc (DVD), and automatic teller machine (ATM) part of our daily lives. Computers and microwaves have become widely used. It is now possible to search thousands of Web sites on a single topic. Fiber-optic cables have improved communication around the world.

Many of us enjoy more comfortable, convenient lives than our parents did. But all this comfort and convenience can distract us from our relationship with God. Our world still faces problems of poverty and injustice. As Christians we are called to care for those who are poor, sick, or suffering.

Our rapidly developing technologies can widen the gap between those who have access to the latest devices and those who do not. Our challenge is to keep our focus on our relationship with God.

Rights Revolution and Nationalism

As the Enlightenment ended in Europe, a period of *revolution* began. During this time, ideas such as freedom of conscience were taken to an extreme by some people. As an example, the leaders of the French Revolution (1789–1799) sought to destroy or disable major institutions, including the Church. By the end of that revolution, the Church in France had lost its property and schools; many of the clergy faithful to Rome had been killed or exiled; religious orders had been disbanded; and all religious activities were banned. Though the revolution led to many social advances for the French people, it also showed how ideas of freedom could be applied destructively.

The revolution in France was followed by struggles in many other countries. It was a time of *nationalism,* when countries began to restructure both their governments and their borders.

The Church took part in these changes, too. For centuries the country that is now Italy had been many separate territories, loosely connected for reasons of trade and defense. The pope had ruled one of these territories, the Papal States. As Italy was united between 1859 and 1870, the Papal States became part of Italy. Today the pope lives in Vatican City, an independent state of about one hundred acres located in the city of Rome. The **College of Cardinals,** a body of cardinals chosen by the pope, meets in Vatican City to advise the pope and to elect the next pope.

Once the Papal States became part of Italy, the Church did not become weaker, as some people had expected. In fact, the Church became stronger because the pope was able to focus on being a spiritual leader. Meanwhile, the telegraph, steamships, and trains were making it possible for news to travel more quickly from Rome to other parts of the world, thereby helping Catholics feel part of a worldwide Church community.

Catholics Believe

Christ has given all of us different gifts so that we can serve the unity and mission of the Church.
See Catechism, #873.

Three gifts that I can share with the

Church right now are _____,

_____, and _____.

Share your responses and thoughts with your Faith Partner.

Seeking Social Justice

As science and technology advanced during the nineteenth century, it became possible to manufacture goods more quickly and inexpensively. This was the beginning of *industrialism.* As factories were built, people moved from farms to cities to get work.

Industrialism made it possible for people to buy things that had not been available earlier. But the growth of industry also brought problems. Factory owners sometimes became wealthy, but their workers were underpaid and worked in dangerous conditions. There was little organized medical care, and people could lose their jobs without warning.

In 1891 Pope Leo XIII wrote *On the Condition of the Working Person* to address the rights of workers and to warn people about the dangers of industrialization. This helped spur many countries to pass laws to ensure that business owners could not overwork, underpay, or abuse their workers, and labor unions flourished.

A World in Pain

The nineteenth and twentieth centuries have witnessed many advances in social justice and freedom. But, as in the case of the French Revolution, ideas of justice and freedom have sometimes been used destructively.

During the Russian Revolution (1917) the czar of Russia and his family were killed. The leaders of the revolution established a new government that was intended to give the people more control. However, the promises made to the people were not kept. One abuse of the new government was to suppress organized religion, including Catholicism.

In Germany, Adolf Hitler and the Nazi party came to power in 1933. Hitler's efforts to conquer much of Europe led to World War II. Hitler and the Nazis were also responsible for the *Holocaust,* the killing of Jewish people, gypsies, homosexuals, and those who were mentally ill or physically disabled. Hitler was stopped, but not before millions of people—including six million Jews—lost their lives.

Even today some countries are ruled by corrupt leaders who order the deaths of innocent people in their attempts at *ethnic cleansing,* the elimination of a whole culture or race from a country.

Opening the Word

Create in me a clean heart, O God, and put a new and right spirit within me. Psalm 51:10

Read *Psalm 51:10–12* as well as *Romans 15:1–6, 1 Corinthians 12:27–30,* and *Ephesians 4:25–29.* Which of the gifts mentioned would help you be a witness to the gospel message?

_____

_____

The Modern Church

In the twentieth century the Catholic Church took advantage of new opportunities to share the gospel message. One outstanding Catholic broadcaster was Bishop Fulton J. Sheen, who shared his message through radio broadcasts that began in 1930 and were expanded into television in 1951. His television show "Life Is Worth Living" won an Emmy before it ended its run in 1957.

Besides enabling the Church to spread its message to a wider audience, technological advances such as radio, television, and now the Internet have allowed people to become more aware of and affected by world events. Wars, famine, social injustice, and political and economic abuses are now harder to ignore. Over the course of the past two centuries, the Church has called two major councils to discuss the issues raised by the modern world.

Vatican I

Between 1869 and 1870 Pius IX called the **First Vatican Council,** the first Church council called since the Council of Trent in the sixteenth century. The main goal of this council was to address the anti-religious views that had developed during the nineteenth century. One of the actions of the council was the declaration of papal **infallibility.** The council declared that when bishops and the pope together (or in some cases, the pope individually) define a doctrine concerning faith and morals *and* declare that they are speaking infallibly, they speak without error. Papal infallibility has very rarely been exercised. In fact, the only case in which a pope has declared a teaching infallible since Vatican I was the 1950 declaration of Mary's Assumption.

Our Global Community

Spreading the Word

One of the great ages of missionary activity was the early twentieth century. Many European and American religious orders sent missionaries to Africa, South and Central America, and countries in the Far East. Missionaries led difficult, lonely, and sometimes heroic lives as they spread the faith and established churches and schools. While some missionaries became overly concerned with political power, most did what they could to share the good news of Jesus, improve living conditions, and protect the rights of people.

Vatican II

By the 1960s the Church determined that another council was necessary to discuss how to spread the gospel message in the modern world. In 1962 Pope John XXIII (1881–1963) convened the **Second Vatican Council,** which met between 1962 and 1965. More than two thousand bishops and other Catholic leaders and theologians from all over the world (as well as observers from many other religions) attended the sessions of the council. The decisions of Vatican II resulted in major changes in the life of the Church.

Decisions made by Vatican II made it possible for the Mass to be celebrated in the language spoken by the people instead of the Latin language. As a result the Mass became more of a community celebration. The bishops encouraged Catholics to study the Bible and participate in the Church's mission. Vatican II taught the importance of religious freedom, and progress was made in overcoming prejudice against Jewish people.

The council also decided that the Church needed to work to unite all Christians in the one and only Church of Christ through **ecumenism.** Since Vatican II much has been accomplished through discussions with other Christians, especially Lutherans, Anglicans (Episcopalians), and members of Orthodox Churches. The decisions of the Second Vatican Council also stressed the importance of working for social justice. They reminded us of our call to lessen human suffering and to make our world aware of the basic dignity and respect that every person deserves.

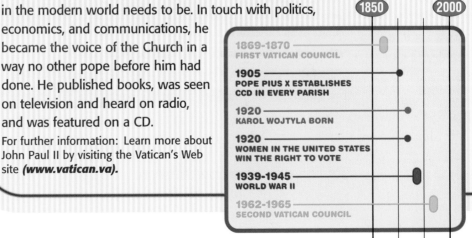

OUR CHRISTIAN JOURNEY

A Voice in the Modern Age When Karol Wojtyla was elected pope in 1978, he was the first non-Italian pope in more than four hundred and fifty years and the first Polish pope. Taking the name John Paul II, he worked to strengthen the unity of the Church and spoke out for justice. Between 1981 and 1991 he published three letters on social justice. He worked to build up the Church in Eastern Europe and was instrumental in the collapse of Communist governments. He traveled to more than 120 countries and was considered a strong media personality. When he was wounded in an assassination attempt in 1981, he publicly forgave his attacker by visiting the man in his prison cell. John Paul II showed what a leader in the modern world needs to be. In touch with politics, economics, and communications, he became the voice of the Church in a way no other pope before him had done. He published books, was seen on television and heard on radio, and was featured on a CD.

For further information: Learn more about John Paul II by visiting the Vatican's Web site (**www.vatican.va**).

1850   2000

1869-1870
FIRST VATICAN COUNCIL

1905
POPE PIUS X ESTABLISHES
CCD IN EVERY PARISH

1920
KAROL WOJTYLA BORN

1920
WOMEN IN THE UNITED STATES
WIN THE RIGHT TO VOTE

1939-1945
WORLD WAR II

1962-1965
SECOND VATICAN COUNCIL

In the Modern World

After a colorful history, the Catholic Church is still a teacher, a healer, and a guide. The people of the Church remind the world of Jesus' teachings and share the word of God with everyone. They seek to heal the brokenness of our world by working for social justice and ecumenism. They also work to heal the brokenness of the Christian community so that all Christians will be united again. Just as the Church guided people in the past, the teachings of the Church guide us today.

Scientific advances and technological inventions are making it easier for people to work and communicate. But it is important for all people to have the chance to share in the progress that technology makes possible. Technology can be a wonderful tool, but even the best tool can be used to harm people. Christ calls us to protect those who are powerless and help those who are in need.

Both faith and technology are needed today to spread the good news of the gospel throughout the world. We are learning that having the technology to do something does not necessarily mean that we should do it. Our world offers us many options. Our relationship with God can help us make wise decisions so that we use the available technologies to do what is right and good.

Reflect on how both faith and technology are part of your life. Share your thoughts with your Faith Partner.

WRAP UP

- Developments in science, technology, and psychology can help us more effectively share the gospel.
- Vatican I decreed the doctrine of infallibility.
- Vatican II helped the Church bring the message of Christ to the modern world.
- The Church encourages ecumenism, which means working for the unity of all Christians.
- The Catholic Church is a strong voice for social justice.
- The Catholic Church has been and is a teacher, healer, and guide.

What questions do you have about the content of this chapter?

_____

_____

_____

Around the Group

Discuss the following question as a group.

What are some examples of the Church being a teacher, a healer, and a guide in the modern world?

After everyone has had a chance to share his or her responses, focus on one aspect and come up with a group answer upon which everyone can agree.

_____

_____

_____

_____

What personal observations do you have about the group discussion and answer?

_____

_____

_____

_____

Briefly...

At the beginning of this chapter, you were asked to consider the usefulness of electronic devices. Which electronic devices could be helpful to the Church as it works to guide or heal the people of the world?

_____

_____

_____

_____

Dealing with Anxiety

Expressions of Faith—

Progress means change, and sometimes change means stress and anxiety. When anxiety overwhelms us, it can be impossible to be kind to others, to be happy, or to lead useful lives. Dealing with Anxiety is an important skill in our lives. The Church calls us to experience God's peace, love, and security in our lives. When we deal with our anxiety, we are better able to live hopeful lives and respond to the needs of others.

Scripture

"Therefore I tell you, do not worry about your life, what you will eat or what you will drink, or about your body, what you will wear. Is not life more than food, and the body more than clothing? Look at the birds of the air; they neither sow nor reap nor gather into barns, and yet your heavenly Father feeds them. Are you not of more value than they? And can any of you by worrying add a single hour to your span of life?"

Matthew 6:25–27 8th Sunday of Ordinary Time, Cycle A

Think About It—

Dealing with anxiety has always been a concern for humans. Jesus made it a point to directly address this concern. Reread *Matthew 6:25–27.*

○ What do you <u>hear</u> in this statement from Jesus?

_____

_____

_____

○ What <u>feeling</u> do you get when you read this passage?

_____

_____

_____

○ What <u>thoughts</u> come to your mind when you read this passage?

_____

_____

_____

Skill Steps-

Dealing with Anxiety is a skill that involves emotional management. You already practiced this skill in Chapters 3 and 4 when you learned how to handle anger. You used the following three steps: Name It, Tame It, and Claim It.

Here are some things to keep in mind about the skill of Dealing with Anxiety.

- Name It: *Identify what is causing the anxiety.* It's important to figure out whether you are concerned about failure, safety, loss, or rejection. Your source of anxiety will almost always be one of these.

- Tame It: *Talk* with someone about what you are thinking and feeling. Use the *talents* God has given you to make things better or to solve the problem. *Trust* that God will help you get through it. He may not help you

avoid it (after all, he didn't spare Jesus from suffering). But he will give you the strength to face it. Then, walk *toward* your anxiety: decide on your own way to handle it and then let go, confident that the wisdom and strength of the Holy Spirit will guide you. Running away from anxiety, denying it, or worrying about it only makes the situation last longer in your mind.

- Claim It: Finally, *realize that you can learn important lessons from the anxiety.* You can learn what usually causes you to experience anxiety. You can learn what works and doesn't work for you in dealing with the emotion. You can learn how talented you are and how much God loves and supports you during anxious times.

Check It Out-

Place a check mark next to the sentences that apply to you.

◯ I don't experience much anxiety.

◯ I know what most often causes me anxiety.

◯ When I'm anxious, I ask God to give me the strength and grace I need to move on.

◯ I know and use several ways to tame my anxiety.

◯ I don't think I've been doing well in dealing with my anxiety.

Based on your responses, what kinds of things would you like to work on?

_____

_____

Closing Prayer-

Lord, help us trust you enough to open our hearts to you. We know that you see us completely, but it can be hard for us to rely on you. Learning to trust is difficult. We are troubled by doubt and confusion. Help us turn to you and depend on you when we are anxious. Amen.

Loving God,
you alone see
the future and
recognize the
joys and
sorrows of our
tomorrows.
Take care of
your Church
and your world.
Hold us close to
your heart, and
make us your
holy people.
Amen.

The Church of the Third Millennium

Why do you think the Church is often described as a community?

_____

_____

Circle the words that you think best describe the Church as an institution and as a people of God.

Church as an Institution	Church as a People of God
holy	holy
united	united
universal	universal
involved	involved
generous	generous
influential	influential
welcoming	welcoming
faithful	faithful
prayerful	prayerful
worshiping	worshiping
caring	caring
political	political
helpful	helpful
promoter of justice	promoter of justice

Belonging

The memories, experiences, and connections that we have with the Church are different for each of us. Memories of special occasions in the Church, such as a First Communion, a family member's wedding, or a funeral, remind us that we are not alone in the world. We belong to the Church, the community of the followers of Jesus Christ, and that community supports us in our life of faith.

We can freely choose to live our personal lives within the larger framework of our Christian story. Just as God worked through people of faith in the past, he works through us today.

The Call to Faith

In the late twentieth century, Catholics could be found throughout the world. The Church was well established in Europe and the Americas, and it was growing quickly in Africa. But in Asia many Christians were facing persecution, and Catholics in Latin America were being challenged by evangelical Christians, who presented a different style of faith. Missionaries in Russia and China often faced the difficulty of spreading the faith in countries where governments were not open to their presence. Catholics in the Middle East were in the minority and faced prejudice and pressures from governments and other religious groups. The Church was called to witness to God's love again and again.

Christians give special significance to the thousand-year periods counted from the birth of Christ. At the beginning of a new **millennium,** the teachings of the Second Vatican Council continue to provide guidance. These teachings remind us that the Church is the whole people of God. We must not depend on the pope, the bishops, or our pastors to be the Church; instead, we must share in the responsibility for learning about our faith and living it. Vatican II also teaches us that the Church must work for peace and justice in the world—both as a community of faith and as individuals. As the Body of Christ, we are called to lead the world in showing respect for the dignity of every person.

Share with your Faith Partner one way that you show respect for other people.

FAiTH PaRTNeRSHiP

Opening the Word

17th Sunday of Ordinary Time, Cycle B

There is one body and one Spirit, just as you were called to the one hope of your calling, one Lord, one faith, one baptism, one God and Father of all, who is above all and through all and in all. Ephesians 4:4–6

Read *Ephesians 4:4–7* as well as *John 14:12* and *1 Corinthians 2:1–5*. How can you as a Christian witness to the power and greatness of God?

_____

_____

_____

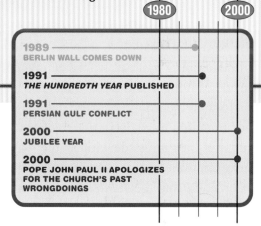

A Letter About Justice The encyclical *The Hundredth Year* was published in 1991 to celebrate the one-hundredth anniversary of *On the Condition of Working People,* an important encyclical about the rights of workers. *The Hundredth Year* points out that the Church does not emphasize specific programs to make life better for those who are suffering. Instead, it calls all of us to respect human dignity in all that we do. Democratic forms of government can help improve things for people, but those who are poor, suffering, or exploited need more than government programs. This encyclical on social justice reminds us of the ideals that give us the wisdom and courage to solve problems in our world.

For further information: Use the Internet to research one of the Church's social justice documents.

1980   **2000**

1989
BERLIN WALL COMES DOWN

1991
THE HUNDREDTH YEAR PUBLISHED

1991
PERSIAN GULF CONFLICT

2000
JUBILEE YEAR

2000
POPE JOHN PAUL II APOLOGIZES FOR THE CHURCH'S PAST WRONGDOINGS

Faith at Work

In the third millennium the Church will need to speak out in many ways. Through its **prophetic** voice, the Church can call people all over the world to holiness. By communicating hopes, promises, and warnings concerning people's relationships with God, the Church is a sign of God's presence and God's love for each person. The Church reminds all Christians that they are accountable to God for how they live.

The Church's witness to the sacredness of life can lead us all to consider how we value life in our homes and communities, as well as in the nation. The issues of abortion and capital punishment challenge us to honor life by making decisions that may be very difficult or unpopular. We need to be sure that our attitudes and actions demonstrate our respect for life as God's gift. Because

God has entrusted us with the *stewardship* of his creation as well, the Church must encourage care for the earth and all the creatures within it. As we follow Jesus' teachings and share what we believe, we encourage others to live moral lives.

The Church's voice of compassion must continue to call our attention to people who are poor, people who have been hurt or abused, and people who are being oppressed. We must show God's love by finding ways to lessen their pain and let them feel God's love in the midst of their struggles. The Church can guide us in being faithful to God as we use our knowledge and technologies to bring about a more just and loving society.

Christ takes care of his Church, acting through it to bring truth and grace to all. See Catechism, #771.

How can the Church bring truth to both Catholics and non-Catholics?

_____

_____

_____

As members of the Church, we must encourage our nation to respond to the needs of developing nations, whose people endure levels of hunger and disease that are hard for us to imagine. Many of these nations have accumulated huge debts that they can never repay if they are to develop stable ways of governing themselves and caring for their people. During the *Jubilee Year 2000,* the bishops of the United States called for national leaders to help resolve the crisis caused by these debts and the difficulty in repaying them.

Accountability
and Healing

We are called to be accountable for our actions, but we are also to forgive one another and work for healing and reconciliation in all aspects of our lives. In recent years the pope and other Church leaders have expressed sorrow for the tragic results of the Crusades and for actions by Catholics over the centuries that have brought pain, separation, and even death to individuals and to entire groups of people. This confession has helped people see that even though we are imperfect and have sinned, we can still address injustices wherever we find them. With God's

grace, we can do much to lessen the effects of evil in our world. God is still present with us, working to perfect the Church.

As Catholics we can reach out to baptized people who have felt disconnected from the Church for various reasons. Some people who are divorced may not feel welcome to participate in the life of the Church. Others may have bad memories of their experience with a particular teacher or priest many years ago. Or perhaps a woman who has had an abortion feels that the Church will not accept her. We can be instruments of God's healing as we reach out to welcome and include them in the community of faith.

You may face situations in which one person labels or harasses another. You may know someone who is being treated badly or even violently. How can you respond as a prophetic Christian in situations like this? It is often not possible and not safe to reason with someone who is involved in violent behavior. But you can talk with a trusted adult friend or mentor about your feelings and what is happening. Together you can work toward what might be done to stop the violence or other hurtful actions. The person responsible for the unacceptable action is also a child of God, but he or she must be held accountable for violent actions.

Your Challenges

You will experience times when you don't want to be generous, when you can't pray, and when you aren't sure what you believe. Everyone experiences such times. Such feelings don't mean that you are a bad person or that your faith isn't real. Maybe God is calling you in a new direction. Continue trying to be a good person, but have compassion for yourself as well as for others. Ask God's help and rely on his grace to support you during those times.

At each stage of your life, you will face challenges and opportunities to live your faith. Both can be seen as God's call to use your gifts and talents. Others your age will also experience this call. In fact, it is very likely that more than one person in your generation will be canonized a saint at some point in the future. These individuals will have lived lives of holiness in new ways. They will be imitated and remembered by generations of future Catholics. Will you know these individuals? Will you be one of them? It's possible. What is certain is that as you faithfully live your personal story, you will discover many ways that your particular gifts contribute to the richness of our Christian story.

care for the environment

respect for life

HUMAN DIGNITY

Media Message

THE ELECTRONIC FUTURE Developments in technology and new forms of media continue to transform our lives and the ways in which we communicate with one another. The remotest parts of the world can now be easily reached by cell phone, fax, and e-mail. This electronic revolution also transforms the way we share our faith. Even the Vatican has its own Web site *(www.vatican.va),* as do many parishes and dioceses.

If you were to design a Web site to share your faith, what would it look like? Sketch or describe what images you would include, what you would say, and what links you would provide.

Making a
Difference

If you could go back in time, when would you most want to live as a Christian? Why? Your answer may lead to some helpful discoveries about your way of living your faith. If you find the Middle Ages appealing, with the beautiful glass, wood, and stone of the great cathedrals, then perhaps you will express your faith through a form of art. Are you fascinated by the lives of the missionaries? Perhaps you have the ability to communicate with others and have a gift for sharing your faith.

Take a close look at your parish. In what activities and events can you participate? Is there a youth ministry with programs, activities, and events? A music or prayer group just for young adolescents? A social concerns committee? Talk with others and decide what you and others your age can do to strengthen your faith and your involvement in the Church's mission. Perhaps you can develop a program, event, or activity that will make a difference for people in your parish. Get other young adolescents and adults involved. Meet with parish leaders and plan what you can do.

Don't wait for the future to live your faith. You can make a difference in your parish and community today. You can rely on God to prompt you to share your gifts and talents. Let your personal story be a vital part of our ongoing Christian story.

If you were going to organize a way for youth to become active in the life of your parish, what would you do? Share your thoughts with your Faith Partner.

FaiTH PaRTNeRSHip

WRAP UP

- Belonging to the Church means loving and serving Christ and others.

- The Church is a prophetic voice in the world for justice and goodness.

- During the third millennium, the Church continues to work so that all humans can come to know and love God.

- You can make a difference in your parish today because you are part of the Church's story.

What questions do you have about the content of this chapter?

_____

_____

_____

Around the Group

List on the board or on chart paper several ways that young adolescents can get involved in their parish community.

After everyone has had a chance to share his or her responses, come up with a group list upon which everyone can agree.

_____

_____

_____

_____

What personal observations do you have about the group discussion and list?

_____

_____

_____

_____

Briefly . . .

At the beginning of this chapter, you were asked to consider words that describe the Church. What words best describe who you are as a member of the Body of Christ?

_____

_____

_____

SKILLS FOR Christian Living

Dealing with Anxiety

Expressions of Faith–

The Church's story is certainly one of faith, but it is also one of hope and fortitude. The Church has persisted through many troubles and trials over two thousand years. As a member of the Body of Christ, you will need the skill of Dealing with Anxiety.

Scripture

Peter answered him, "Lord, if it is you, command me to come to you on the water." He said, "Come." So Peter got out of the boat, started walking on the water, and came toward Jesus. But when he noticed the strong wind, he became frightened, and beginning to sink, he cried out, "Lord, save me!"

Matthew 14:28–30

19th Sunday of Ordinary Time, Cycle A

Skill Steps–

Dealing with Anxiety is a skill that needs to be practiced. Review the Name It, Tame It, and Claim It steps in Chapter 9.

Here are some things to remember as you practice this skill:

- Dealing with anxiety has been a concern for people throughout history.
- Jesus spoke to his followers about dealing with anxiety.
- Every Mass includes a prayer for God's help in dealing with anxiety.
- Our personal stories call for the same kind of perseverance, faith, and hope that the Church has shown throughout anxious times in our Christian story.

Skill Builder–

Recall a situation that caused you a lot of anxiety within the last year. Review the situation in light of the three steps (Name It, Tame It, Claim It).

Circle the source of worry that caused your anxiety at that time.

failure   safety   loss   rejection

- What did you do about your anxiety? Did you talk, use your talents, trust God, walk toward the anxiety? How?

_____

- What did you learn from that experience?

_____

Putting It into Practice-

We can learn from the experiences of others what they do to deal with anxiety; however, it is equally important that we look at our own experiences and practice what we have learned. Complete the following using the method Name It, Tame It, Claim It.

Think about something that is currently causing you anxiety.

○ Name It: **What is the source of your worry: failure, safety, loss, or rejection?**

_____

_____

○ Tame It: **Evaluate using the following questions:**

To whom can you talk? _____

_____

What talents can help you deal with this situation? _____

_____

What do you need to trust God to do? _____

_____

What concrete action will help you walk toward your anxiety and deal with it? _____

_____

○ Claim It: **Based on what you have learned in the past, what do you think you can learn from this experience of anxiety?**

_____

_____

By taking time to describe what you are feeling, you will help keep yourself from adding more anxiety. Deciding what positive action you can take is a way of putting your anxiety to good use.

Now that you have had some practice in naming, taming, and claiming your anxiety, list below one aspect of this skill that you are good at and one that you still need to work on.

_____

_____

Closing Prayer-

*Lord of all, **teach** us to lead prophetic lives. Grant us the wisdom to recognize injustice and the **desire** to spread truth. Give us the courage to speak your word and to work for justice. Amen.*

Prayers and
Resources

The Lord's Prayer

Our Father, who art in heaven,
hallowed be thy name;
thy kingdom come;
thy will be done on earth as it is in heaven.
Give us this day our daily bread;
and forgive us our trespasses
as we forgive those who trespass against us;
and lead us not into temptation,
but deliver us from evil.
Amen.

Hail Mary

Hail, Mary, full of grace,
the Lord is with you!
Blessed are you among women,
and blessed is the fruit of your womb, Jesus.
Holy Mary, Mother of God,
pray for us sinners,
now and at the hour of our death.
Amen.

THE TEN COMMANDMENTS

1. I am the Lord your God. You shall not have strange gods before me.

2. You shall not take the name of the Lord your God in vain.

3. Remember to keep holy the Lord's day.

4. Honor your father and your mother.

5. You shall not kill.

6. You shall not commit adultery.

7. You shall not steal.

8. You shall not bear false witness against your neighbor.

9. You shall not covet your neighbor's wife.

10. You shall not covet your neighbor's goods.

THE BEATITUDES

Blessed are the poor in spirit,
    for theirs is the kingdom
    of heaven.

Blessed are they who mourn,
    for they will be comforted.

Blessed are the meek,
    for they will inherit the land.

Blessed are they who hunger and
thirst for righteousness,
    for they will be satisfied.

Blessed are the merciful,
    for they will be shown mercy.

Blessed are the clean of heart,
    for they will see God.

Blessed are the peacemakers,
    for they will be called children
    of God.

Blessed are they who are persecuted
for the sake of righteousness,
    for theirs is the kingdom
    of heaven.

(Matthew 5:3–10)

Glory to the Father (Doxology)

Glory to the Father, and to the Son,
and to the Holy Spirit:
as it was in the beginning, is now,
and will be for ever.
Amen.

Gifts of the Holy Spirit

Wisdom
Understanding
Right judgment (Counsel)
Courage (Fortitude)
Knowledge
Reverence (Piety)
Wonder and awe (Fear of the Lord)

Fruits of the Spirit

Charity
Joy
Peace
Patience
Kindness
Goodness
Generosity
Gentleness
Faithfulness
Modesty
Self-control
Chastity

Act of Contrition

My God,
I am sorry for my sins with all my
heart.
In choosing to do wrong
and failing to do good,
I have sinned against you
whom I should love above all things.
I firmly intend, with your help,
to do penance,
to sin no more,
and to avoid whatever leads me to sin.
Our Savior Jesus Christ
suffered and died for us.
In his name, my God, have mercy.

Works of Mercy

Corporal (for the body)
Feed the hungry.
Give drink to the thirsty.
Clothe the naked.
Shelter the homeless.
Visit the sick.
Visit the imprisoned.
Bury the dead.

Spiritual (for the spirit)
Warn the sinner.
Teach the ignorant.
Counsel the doubtful.
Comfort the sorrowful.
Bear wrongs patiently.
Forgive injuries.
Pray for the living and the dead.

PRECEPTS OF THE CHURCH

1. Take part in the Mass on Sundays and holy days. Keep these days holy and avoid unnecessary work.

2. Celebrate the Sacrament of Reconciliation at least once a year if there is serious sin.

3. Receive Holy Communion at least once a year during Easter time.

4. Fast and abstain on days of penance.

5. Give your time, gifts, and money to support the Church.

The Apostles' Creed

I believe in God, the Father almighty,
  creator of heaven and earth.
I believe in Jesus Christ, his only Son,
  our Lord.
  He was conceived by the power of the
    Holy Spirit
    and born of the Virgin Mary.
  He suffered under Pontius Pilate,
    was crucified, died, and was buried.
  He descended to the dead.
  On the third day, he rose again.
He ascended into heaven,
  and is seated at the right hand
    of the Father.
He will come again to judge the
  living and the dead.
I believe in the Holy Spirit,
  the holy catholic Church,
  the communion of saints,
  the forgiveness of sins,
  the resurrection of the body,
  and life everlasting. Amen.

The Nicene Creed

We believe in one God,
  the Father, the Almighty,
  maker of heaven and earth,
  of all that is, seen and unseen.
We believe in one Lord, Jesus Christ,
  the only Son of God,
  eternally begotten of the Father,
  God from God, Light from Light,
  true God from true God,
  begotten, not made, one in Being
    with the Father.
  Through him all things were made.
  For us men and for our salvation
    he came down from heaven:
  by the power of the Holy Spirit
    he was born of the Virgin Mary,
    and became man.
  For our sake he was crucified under
    Pontius Pilate;
  he suffered, died, and was buried.
  On the third day he rose again
    in fulfillment of the Scriptures;
he ascended into heaven
  and is seated at the right hand
    of the Father.
He will come again in glory to judge
  the living and the dead,
  and his kingdom will have no end.
We believe in the Holy Spirit, the Lord,
  the giver of life,
  who proceeds from the Father and
    the Son.
  With the Father and the Son he is
    worshiped and glorified.
  He has spoken through the Prophets.
We believe in one holy catholic and
  apostolic Church.
We acknowledge one baptism for the
  forgiveness of sins.
We look for the resurrection
  of the dead,
  and the life of the world to come.
Amen.

The Liturgical Year

In the liturgical year the Church celebrates Jesus' life, death, resurrection, and ascension through its seasons and holy days. The liturgical year begins with the First Sunday of Advent.

The readings for the entire Church year are contained in the Lectionary. Readings for Sundays and solemnities of the Lord are placed in a three-year rotation—Cycle A, Cycle B, and Cycle C.

The Season of Advent begins in late November or early December. During Advent we recall the first coming of the Son of God into human history, and we prepare for the coming of Christ—in our hearts, in history, and at the end of time. The liturgical color for Advent is violet.

On Christmas we celebrate the Incarnation, the Son of God becoming one of us. The color for Christmas is white, a symbol of celebration and life in Christ. (Any time white is used, gold may be used.)

Lent is the season of prayer and sacrifice that begins with Ash Wednesday and lasts about forty days. Lent has always been a time of repentance through prayer, fasting, and almsgiving. The liturgical color for Lent is purple, a symbol of penance.

Easter is the high point of the liturgical year because it celebrates Jesus' resurrection from the dead. The week beginning with Palm Sunday is called Holy Week. Lent ends on Holy Thursday evening, when the Easter Triduum begins. The Triduum, or "three holy days," includes the observance of Holy Thursday, Good Friday, and the Easter Vigil on Holy Saturday. The liturgical color for the Easter Season is white, a symbol of our joy in experiencing new life in Christ. The Easter Season lasts about seven weeks (fifty days).

At Pentecost, we celebrate the gift of the Holy Spirit sent to the followers of Jesus gathered in the upper room in Jerusalem. The liturgical color for Pentecost is red, a symbol of the tongues as of fire on Pentecost and of how Christ and some of his followers (such as the early Christian martyrs) sacrificed their lives for love of God.

The majority of the liturgical year is called Ordinary Time, a time when the Church community reflects on what it means to walk in the footsteps of Jesus. The liturgical color for Ordinary Time is green, a symbol of hope and growth.

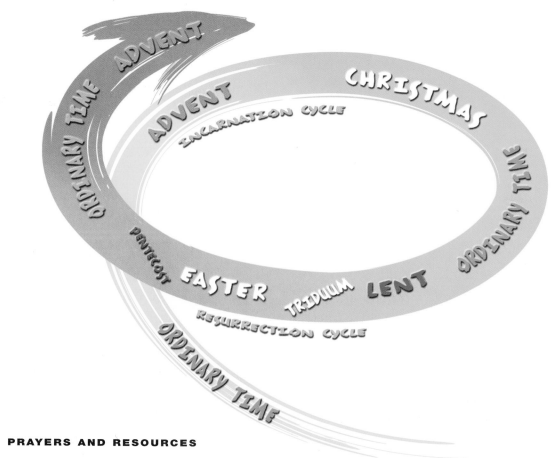

Glossary

A apostles — Twelve friends and followers of Jesus to whom he entrusted his mission. The number of apostles corresponds to the number of tribes of Israel.

Apostles' Creed — A formal statement based on the beliefs of the apostles.

apostolic succession — The process by which bishops in every age are given the authority to carry out their work of shepherding the Church.

C catholic — Universal; the Church is catholic because its mission is to the whole world.

Christianity — The religion of those who follow Jesus Christ and his teachings.

Church — The community of believers who gather to hear the word of God and be nourished with the Eucharist and in that way become the Body of Christ.

Church fathers — Early Church leaders who devoted a significant part of their ministry to building up the Body of Christ by teaching the faith of the apostles, helping people grow into the fullness of the Christian life, and protecting the Church against heresy.

College of Cardinals — The organized body of cardinals of the Catholic Church who elect a new pope.

Council of Jerusalem — A Church council held in A.D. 49 to debate whether or not Gentiles who became Christians would be required to follow all Jewish laws.

Council of Trent — A council of the Church that met between 1545 and 1563 to deal with issues raised by the Reformation.

D diocese — A Catholic community, usually described by its geographical location or boundaries, which is entrusted to the pastoral care of a bishop.

disciple — A person who accepts, lives, and spreads the teachings of another.

E East-West Schism — The split between the Eastern and Western Church around 1054 because of differences in doctrine, culture, politics, authority, and language.

ecumenism — The spirit that motivates Christians to come together cooperatively and look forward to a time of unity for Christians in the one and only Church of Christ.

Enlightenment — A movement of the eighteenth century that emphasized the use of reason in solving problems and gaining knowledge.

Eucharist — The sacrament of Jesus' presence, which we celebrate by receiving his own Body and Blood under the form of bread and wine at Mass. From the Greek word meaning "gratitude," or "thanksgiving."

evangelization — Giving witness to our faith by proclaiming the good news of Jesus Christ through our words and actions.

F First Vatican Council — A council that convened in 1869 to combat political and religious ideas of the time that were calling into question the authority of the Church and of the Christian faith itself.

G Gentile — A term used by Jewish people to describe a person of non-Jewish faith or origin.

gospel — The good news of God's saving love. The first four books of the New Testament, which present Jesus' teachings, are called the Gospels.

Great Western Schism — The split in the Church in the West, from 1378 to 1417, because of a disagreement between bishops about the election of popes. The dispute was resolved by a decision of the Council of Constance.

H humanism — A way of life that stresses individual dignity and worth.

I indulgence — A sharing in the fruits of Jesus' saving action; understood as a reduction of temporal punishment for sin, through prayer and other good works done out of faith.

infallibility — A charism given by Christ to the pope, and to the bishops in union with the pope, by which they speak without error on certain matters regarding faith and morals.

J justification by faith — The belief that we are saved by our faith in Jesus Christ and that no effort of ours can earn our salvation.

L lay missionary — A Catholic who works in a missionary setting but is not ordained or is not a full member of a religious community.

M martyr — A saint or other holy person who witnessed to Christ and was killed because he or she was a follower of Jesus or because he or she upheld a Christian value.

Middle Ages — The period of European history from about A.D. 500 to 1500.

millennium — A period of a thousand years; Christians give special significance to the thousand-year periods counted from the birth of Christ.

missionary — One who is sent to carry the good news of God's kingdom to other people, often in circumstances or cultures other than one's own.

monasticism — A way of life followed by religious who live apart from the larger society, either singly or in community, according to a rule of life and under vows, in order to give themselves more fully to God's service.

mystic — A person who devotes his or her life to contemplation. Mystics are sometimes led to a deep communion with God and may be given visions of his kingdom.

N New Testament — The fulfillment of the Old Covenant; the second part of the Bible, which contains the four Gospel accounts of Jesus and his followers, the Acts of the Apostles, several letters, and the Book of Revelation.

P parish — A defined community of Catholic faithful within a specific geographical portion of a diocese, which is entrusted to the pastoral care of a priest, or pastor.

Pentecost — The descent of the Holy Spirit upon the apostles fifty days after Easter. The word *Pentecost* means "the fiftieth day."

persecution — The effort by one group to suppress or hinder the freedom of another group by harming or threatening its members.

prophetic — Speaking the truth; communicating hopes, promises, and warnings concerning people's relationships with God and with one another.

Protestant — A person of the sixteenth century who protested the Catholic Church's teachings and practices and who sought to reform Christianity by breaking away from the Catholic Church.

R Reformation — The sixteenth-century call for reform within the Catholic Church that resulted in the formation of Christian Churches not in union with the Catholic Church.

Renaissance — A period from the fourteenth to the seventeenth centuries A.D., during which many Europeans rediscovered the writings of the ancient Greeks and Romans and began to use them as their models for learning, art, and architecture.

S saint — A holy person; one whose life exemplifies holiness and dedication to God.

Second Vatican Council — A council that convened in 1962 to help the Church define its role in the modern world.

U universality — A quality of existing everywhere, within all cultural patterns, and being open to everyone.

W word of God — God's revelation of himself, which nourishes and strengthens the Church. Scripture, which was inspired by the Holy Spirit, is the word of God and Christ is the living Word of God.